STUDYING FILMS

ALSO AVAILABLE IN THIS SERIES

STUDYING HOT FUZZ
Neil Archer

Dedication and acknowledgements

To the film students at Keele, to my colleagues, and (as ever) to G & N.

Thanks also to my editor, John Atkinson, for his relentless enthusiasm.

First published in 2015 by
Auteur, 24 Hartwell Crescent, Leighton Buzzard LU7 1NP
www.auteur.co.uk

Copyright © Auteur Publishing 2015

Designed and set by Nikki Hamlett at Cassels Design www.casselsdesign.co.uk

Printed and bound by CPI Group (UK) Ltd, Croydon, CR0 4YY

British Library Cataloguing-in-Publication Data
A catalogue record for this book is available from the British Library

ISBN: 978-0-9932384-0-6 paperback
ISBN: 978-0-9932384-1-3 ebook

Contents

Contents

Introduction: Beyond a Joke?

Fig 1: *UK poster for* Hot Fuzz

It's February 2007, a city in East Anglia. The worst of the English winter is on its way out, and the first sunny inklings of spring are making themselves felt. Every Monday afternoon I catch a bus from outside the Vue cinema, situated in one of the city's shopping centres, on the way to a neighbouring village where I work. While I wait for the bus this particular day, as usual, I browse the cinema's posters and other publicity for new or forthcoming movies. On this Monday I notice, with a significant amount of interest, a large image of the actors Simon Pegg and Nick Frost, their faces separated by the barrel of a conspicuously large gun, the lower part of the picture emblazoned with the name of their new movie: *Hot Fuzz* [Fig 1]. I remember thinking how smart and funny this poster was: vulgar and silly, but also somehow perceptive. Of what, exactly, I wasn't sure, but I wanted to work it out.

Superficially, it looked like any other glossy poster or hoarding you saw in a UK cinema that February. But I'm sure only this one made me smile. It might have been the surprise of seeing the two slightly shambolic stars of *Shaun of the Dead* (2004) and the television series *Spaced* (Channel 4, 1999–2001) with aviator shades and toothpicks, photographed in a way more familiar from images of Hollywood stars such as Bruce Willis or Sylvester Stallone. It might also have been the crude, possibly dubious but also clever play on words so confidently placed as the tagline of the image: 'THEY ARE GOING TO BUST YOUR ARSE.' Or maybe, and most of all, it was the sense of seeing such a knowingly imitative, knowingly bombastic image placed somewhere so undramatic, so *English*, as this East Anglian city, on the road to the Park and Ride, on the way to and from a village with an unpronounceable name. Whatever it was, the seeds of this book were planted at that very moment.

Like many people I came to *Hot Fuzz* having seen *Shaun of the Dead* three years previously. As I remember it, *Shaun* had an unexpected amount of publicity for what was, essentially, a debut film for its director, Edgar Wright,[1] and a first major film role for its lead actor, Simon Pegg. *Shaun of the Dead* was of course helped along by its very astute titular reference to George Romero's classic *Dawn of the Dead* (1975), though what was interesting here was not the reference point itself, but the specifically local spin put on it; the unlikely nature of a zombie movie whose hero was called Shaun, let alone one named after him. *Shaun of the Dead* also made clever use of its setting as part of the publicity drive around the film, putting mock-ups of Pegg's eponymous hero, competing for space with blank-eyed zombies, inside London's phone boxes. This is a publicity practice often informally seen as a desperate publicity bid on the part of hopeless films, but one which here seemed quite apt, given the way the film made use of the same spaces: in this case, various parts of North London, where *Shaun* was largely filmed and set.

My anticipation of *Shaun of the Dead*, and my first viewing of it, were in fact mostly shaped by my own memory of living in London (not far, in fact, from the film's locations), and my still-regular visits to Kentish Town, where my brother lived, and where I saw the film for the first time. Notably, this was on DVD; though like many other people born after the 1960s, I don't see such an important distinction, in terms of what we still rather vaguely call 'the cinematic experience', between home viewing and big-screen exhibition. Watching *Shaun of the Dead* one autumn evening in 2004, with the rattle of the trains passing through Gospel Oak station in the background, joins a long list of cinematic experiences set firmly within the often questionable comforts of various flats, bed-sits and student houses. Significantly, this image from my own memory was one that came back to me when I eventually saw *Hot Fuzz*; more specifically, in what is for me one of the film's defining sequences, when the two policemen played by Pegg and Frost fall asleep over cans of lager and a DVD of *Bad Boys II* (2003).

My final recollection: it's a seasonably warm Wednesday in July, 2013. I am walking down from my house to the Staffordshire town at the foot of the hill. I have a rare free afternoon, the sun is shining, so naturally I head to the local multiplex to see *Pacific Rim* (2013), in which piloted metallic giants fight massive lizards from another dimension. This particular Vue cinema fits snugly into one of the town's few commercial streets, just up the road from my nearest Morrison's supermarket. I spurn the option to browse for bargain Xbox purchases at the Game store on the corner, and resist the familiar, fragrant lure of McDonalds, deciding instead to go straight in to the coolness of the multiplex concourse. What I see as I enter brings back into mind the two memories I've just tried, to the best of my abilities, to evoke; as hanging above my head, over the familiar concession stands for buttery popcorn and cheesy nachos, are once again the faces of Pegg and Frost to promote their new film *The World's End* (2013): the long-awaited third film in the promised trilogy that began, nine years previously, with *Shaun of the Dead*.

More than a sense of anticipation for *The World's End*, what I experienced most of all here was a confirmation of what I'd sensed in 2004, and then, most clearly, outside the East Anglian shopping centre in 2007. What I realised (and here, I trust you will see, is the point of this extended anecdote) is that a film like *Hot Fuzz*, in various ways that I will go on to consider, expresses a great deal about our experience of *watching movies* – as much, if not more, than it is about any 'world' the film supposedly depicts. It's also a film that, in keeping with the initial impression provided by its poster, is at once daft and crude, confident and knowing, but also keenly aware of its time and place. In short: *Hot Fuzz* felt to me in 2007, and still feels today, a very 'British' – or perhaps more accurately 'English' – film experience. What that actually means needs to be considered. A central argument in this book will be that *Hot Fuzz* is not just an example of what we still (rightly or wrongly) call 'British national cinema'. My point will be that the film is in so many ways *about* this idea: what a 'national cinema' means, how we identify it, but also whether and why we actually *need* it.

All this might seem to suggest that *Hot Fuzz* is only really meaningful to viewers who live in strangely-named English villages, or in provincial towns where modern multiplexes nestle between chain stores and supermarkets. If money does indeed talk, box office receipts appear to say a similar thing: *Hot Fuzz* clearly had appeal in its country of origin, making over £20 million at the UK box office. Given that most Hollywood blockbusters spend more than that on marketing (or their stars' salaries) alone, this might not seem much, but we should put it into the perspective not just of a country the size of Great Britain, but also in light of the film's relatively modest production budget (£8 million). Most of all, we should understand this success within the terms of a British cinema market that consistently prefers Hollywood films. *Hot Fuzz*'s UK showing actually compares favourably to the more obvious blockbuster fare from the same year, such as *The Bourne Ultimatum* and *Transformers*, and it even out-performed the fourth installment in the *Die Hard* saga. The fifth *Harry Potter* movie aside (and exactly how 'British' these films are remains a moot point), *Hot Fuzz*'s status as the UK's favourite home-grown film of the year was only challenged by the rubber-faced charms of Rowan Atkinson in *Mr Bean's Holiday*.

One of the interesting things about *Hot Fuzz*, though, is that it was also a very popular movie worldwide, at least given the expectations of a British film internationally. In the American market, which remains the inevitable marker of success for English-language cinema, the film did pretty well, opening in April 2007 across over eight hundred screens and building to a gross of $23 million. Notably, the film did consistently good and even business across the first four weeks of its run: in an age in which movies can live and frequently die in the space of an opening weekend, this would suggest *Hot Fuzz*, for a month at least, fed on positive reviews and word of mouth.

Whichever side of the Atlantic you might hail from (or any other body of water, for that matter), if you're reading this book it's probably because you like this film. In case you're wondering, or worried, I like it too – a lot – and one of the aims of this book is to work out what makes viewers like it so much. There may be any number of reasons for this, though it's probably safe to say that its 'Englishness' is one part of its appeal, whichever way you choose to see it. Maybe your relationship to the film is one of familiarity; from another perspective, the same sources of familiarity for some – English villages, plodding policemen, popular faces from British film and television – might be irresistibly exotic to others. Maybe you like *Hot Fuzz* because you liked *Shaun of the Dead* and *Spaced*. Whatever the reason, trying to work out the appeal of a film like *Hot Fuzz* almost inevitably, at some point, touches upon what we might call its cultural specificity. This sense of being culturally specific, which means not being the same as everything else, explains the appeal of many things, including some people's tastes in movies. But there are also important questions of identity involved in these cultural choices, as these say a lot about who we are, or at least who we want to be; with whom, and with what values and ideas, we wish to identify ourselves.

A main argument in this book is that this sense of identification is central to the experience, and also understanding, of *Hot Fuzz*. If this sounds an unnecessarily earnest task for a book about such a 'fun' film, let me just say at this point that it will hopefully make more sense as we go along. For the moment, though, and as a starting point, think about how much our enthusiasm for *Hot Fuzz* might be informed as much by what it *is not* as what it supposedly is. Let's go back to that publicity image I described previously. If, like me, you are amused by this poster, it might relate to your familiarity with the two actors. But this in itself only partly explains why it's funny. I may have been predisposed to laugh, having enjoyed *Spaced* and *Shaun of the Dead*, but what actually made me laugh was the image of Pegg and Frost in this particular pose. Arguably such a pose is already ridiculous, but it's the unlikely quality – or, to use a word I will return to in this book, the *incongruity* – of putting Pegg and Frost in such a pose that makes it funny. What we see here, in fact, is the work of parody; possibly the most important critical concept for the study of this film, and one I will be exploring in some detail.

That *Hot Fuzz* engages comically with American movies, the movies that traditionally dominate international cinema screens – the kinds of films with which, in the foyer of a UK multiplex, *Hot Fuzz* would be competing for attention – is arguably the most common perception of the film, and its publicity seems to promote this idea. In actuality, this is only part of the story, as many of the more perceptive critical responses to the film indicated. Yet the conception of *Hot Fuzz* as either a 'parody' or 'spoof' of American action cinema is a key feature in various reviews of the film, not just from the UK.[2] This is highlighted by the specific references to such movies, most obviously films like *Point Break* (1991) and *Bad Boys II*, that are explicitly shown and discussed. But above all, it is indicated by the extended action sequence towards the end of the film, when its unlikely action heroes, Nicholas Angel (Pegg) and Danny Butterman (Frost), in critic Peter Bradshaw's words, 'bring [a] wholesomely unreflective American armed response to the English village green'.[3]

As the example of the poster shows, and as the climactic action sequence explores, parody typically works by exploiting, and playing with, our knowledge of a certain text or convention. The parody text acknowledges this convention or previous text, but deviates from the norm sufficiently to make us recognise the difference. The aim of this practice is often to highlight the familiar or clichéd nature of representation: this explains the success of a film franchise like the *Scary Movie* series (2000–2013), which plays, amongst other things, on the frequently predictable nature of the horror genre. Alternatively, parody can be used to highlight the oddity or absurdity of putting one thing – an actor, say, or a location – into a different generic context. Putting the two seemingly unlikely things together (what I will call here 'incongruous juxtaposition') often produces the laughter that is for many the point and pleasure of parody. But it's worth pointing out that even here there is a *critical* element to the parody, drawing attention as it does to the way certain forms of representation, such as film genres, belong in certain contexts, and by implication, others don't.

The UK poster for *Hot Fuzz* works by asking us to recognise its stars from an earlier context, or at least to identify them as British (that is, not from 'Hollywood'). Pegg and Frost's less-than-typical Hollywood looks – for whatever historical, cultural and largely prejudicial reasons – do not link the actors instinctively to the action star status their pose otherwise suggests. The joke here, though, is arguably as much on the macho genre conventions that would exclude them. This is emphasised by the upright gun, possibly a visual allusion to a poster for *Magnum Force* (1973), the second film starring Clint Eastwood as 'Dirty' Harry Callahan, showing Eastwood holding a huge weapon with its barrel pointing upward. The compensatory, psychological connotations of Harry's enormous gun hardly need stressing, though the *Hot Fuzz* image goes all the way here by articulating what the Eastwood image only hints at (what parody theorists call 'literalisation'): in this case, by the highly suggestive pun on cop speak: *They are going to bust your arse.*

This is arguably such an outrageous and silly play on words – the very British use of 'arse' is the killer touch – that the line just manages to get around its dubiously violent sexual associations. In fact, as I'll discuss later, such masculine and at the same time homoerotic subtexts are very much part of *Hot Fuzz*'s parodic target. And many viewers coming to the film, possibly via this poster, and recognising the humour at work, might enjoy this sense of being in on the joke. Parody film encourages strong senses of identification in this way, often by allowing viewers to exercise their film knowledge and critical skill, and thereby feel connected to the parodists: in this case, primarily, Pegg and Frost, and by implication the director Edgar Wright, who (as in *Shaun of the Dead*) also co-wrote the script with Pegg. The local inflections at work here – the British appearance and uniforms, the use of 'arse' – are at once used to deflect familiar and perhaps worn-out conventions, but also to colour our impression of the film within a very English idiom.

Once more, I'm not implying that this is only explicable to the film's 'domestic' audience, as this would underestimate the appeal of British comedy – and in particular, the fun to be had with British English – in successfully exported shows like *Blackadder*, *Monty Python's Flying Circus* and *Fawlty Towers* (we might recall Basil Fawlty's very British attempts, in the episode 'Waldorf Salad', to render *Hot Fuzz's* later tagline: 'I'm going to break your bottom!'). Interestingly, though, where much of the UK publicity worked around the English contexts of the film (in the poster described above, you can see a village reflected in the sunglasses; an alternative poster has this village visible in the background, and in both the latter and other images Frost is wearing a British policeman's helmet), the US and other overseas publicity focused more on the movies that, presumably, were the targets of *Hot Fuzz's* parody. One poster for the American release has the two stars with shotguns and shades, the engulfing fireball behind them echoing familiar action-genre conventions [Fig 2], and perhaps more specifically, a similar publicity image for *Bad Boys II*, with its stars Will Smith and Martin Lawrence sauntering in the foreground. The more straightforward (and, let's face it, uninspired) tagline for this image – *They're Bad Boys. They're Die Hards. They're Lethal Weapons. They are... Hot Fuzz* – suggests that for an American audience the film was being positioned very much in line with other parody films making comedy out of pre-existent movies and franchises. This puts *Hot Fuzz* in line with what film parody expert Dan Harries identifies as a significant and increasingly lucrative trend in recent Hollywood; one initiated by films such as *Airplane!* (1980) and *The Naked Gun* (1988), though more consistently mined by series like the aforementioned *Scary Movie* films, or the two *Hot Shots!* movies (1991, 1993).[4]

Fig 2: US poster for Hot Fuzz

In either case, *Hot Fuzz* appeals to an idea of difference. We can read this in terms of nationality, recognising the film as a *British* movie, not an American one. Alternatively, or even at the same time, we can see it in terms of what some academics have called 'cultural capital', or what we might more informally call the film's *coolness*: the identification of the film as knowingly distinct, irreverent and playful with the films and conventions it references. But here, as they say, is the thing: identifying, and identifying with, the film's coolness and difference also involves some recognition of those same things it is different from. I'm not sure whether having seen *Bad Boys II* makes an appreciable difference to your experience of *Hot Fuzz* (though as I'll explore later, if you have no obvious frame of reference for the supposed parody of *Hot Fuzz*, it begs the question of what it is you are laughing at). We can assume though – and there is plenty of evidence both in the film and in discussions around it to suggest this is the case – that the makers of the film invested considerable attention to watching, using and referencing aspects of action cinema during *Hot Fuzz*'s production. In the same way that the publicity images for the film make use of familiar photographic and compositional elements, the film itself is closely tied at the level of form and content to the genre it is parodying.

The academic Richard Dyer has suggested that parody is in fact 'hysterical', by which he does not necessarily mean funny.[5] What Dyer is pointing out is the ambiguous way parody seems both to embrace and reject its targets: the way it can almost obsessively imitate the smallest details of an earlier text, only then to apparently push it away through moments of deviation or exaggeration (what we informally call 'sending up' or 'spoofing'). Other writers on film have used the term 'loving mockery' to describe this double-edged sense of how parody works.[6] I personally find this kind of label unsatisfying, given its oddly schizophrenic implications, and I believe it is problematic in many ways to attribute it to

Hot Fuzz. Dyer's point nevertheless has significant implications, not just for how we read parody films, but for how we understand our relationship to them; especially, here, if it turns out we ourselves have a 'hysterical' investment in the very films *Hot Fuzz* is parodically referencing. As we'll see, the film may ask us to think carefully about what we regard and what we dismiss in cinematic terms.

Whether we think of *Hot Fuzz* as a jokey cousin to the US action movie or its distant enemy, the idea that parody film is in many instances quite close to its targets, even in terms of production scale, invites us to think carefully about the distance between – in this instance – 'British' and 'Hollywood' cinema. My opening anecdotes were intended to evoke the discrepancy between the shiny lure of Hollywood spectacle and the physical reality of going to the cinema in the UK: a discrepancy that was already acknowledged and displayed in *Hot Fuzz*'s poster parody. The unlikely nature of a Hollywood-style action adventure taking place in a British village is of course the central comic conceit of the film, but as this book will explore, there is something of a paradox at work here. As much as *Hot Fuzz* plays off the comic juxtapositions of genre and British location – a 'big' film in a 'small' location, the action movie on the village green – the film, I will argue, does not revel in its smallness.

One of the more understated and overlooked aspects of *Hot Fuzz* is how deft it is at depicting English space and our relationship to it. But this is not wholeheartedly celebratory; far from it. I'll touch on this at more length later, but the early sequence, where Pegg's newly-promoted Sergeant Angel leaves London for Gloucestershire, is a particularly useful example of this aspect of the film. In a montage of quickly edited shots we see Pegg's character, carrying only a suitcase and his Japanese peace lily, shunted from taxi to train, from railway platform to another train, and finally to another taxi that carries him into the village. Pegg's Sergeant is here a passive and solitary figure, alternately rocked by the movement of the train and an immobile witness to the road signs – 'Welcome to Sandford', 'Model Village' – fleetingly illuminated by the taxi's moving headlights. Punctuating all this is a brilliant piece of narrative economy, as we see the signal on Angel's mobile phone decrease and then flatline: a visual shorthand for loneliness and physical isolation.

Note here that, at this point in the film, 'the country' is a negative place, an imposed and dispiriting removal rather than a happy retreat. Appropriately, this is conveyed through the viewpoint of technological connectivity; a very modern take on the traditional ideas of community, but nevertheless one most of us share or at least understand, and one which certainly reflects the time and place in which *Hot Fuzz* is set (even if Angel's phone already looks a museum piece to most people under eighteen). The tension here between a global, technological currency and older, rural values (consider the dark, creaky oak textures of Pegg's hotel, where his room is named the 'Castle Suite') turns out to be a central one in the film, as I will suggest; but it is also a neat summary of how the film itself lines up, a global product for local audiences who are themselves globally connected through various technologies and media forms.

Also, as I will argue, *Hot Fuzz* is characterised by a stylistic, and also technical, verve and confidence more in keeping with its status as a 'global' film. We can see this in the sequence described above, in the speed and efficiency of its storytelling. It's also worth pointing out that by the time *Hot Fuzz* went into production, its co-writer and star had already had a prominent supporting role in a Hollywood blockbuster (in J.J. Abrams' *Mission: Impossible III*, 2006), and its director would shortly go on to make a critically praised, if financially unsuccessful, big-budget Hollywood movie (2010's *Scott Pilgrim vs. The World*). *Hot Fuzz* is in this respect already halfway to Hollywood, rather than a move in the other direction.

But it was also made at a time when belief in the quality and commercial clout of British filmmaking was high. As Bradshaw put it at the beginning of his *Guardian* review of *Hot Fuzz*, 'There's such euphoria surrounding our film industry right now that I'd be tempted to compare it with the heady days of Britpop'.[7] This connection to the mid-1990s music scene, that saw the rise, amongst many other things, of Blur, Pulp and Oasis, is an interesting one: for me, *Hot Fuzz* shares some of the vigour, but also the interest in exploring ideas of Britishness/Englishness, that characterise some of the music of that period. But it was also a period when British movies, it seemed, could confidently compete internationally in terms both of quality and box-office performance. Suffice it to say this hasn't always been the case for British films, which have often looked to forge an identity not only with regard to their different content, but in terms of a more specifically 'small' style and scale. Simon Pegg's background, chronicled in his 2010 autobiography *Nerd Do Well*, is interesting in this respect: as a child of the 1970s, he grew up during what is often seen as the most lamentable decade for British cinema, though for children, especially, something of a golden age in American film and television. It's not within the scope or focus of this book to suggest why this was – global economics had quite a bit to do with it – but late 1970s Britain presents itself to our contemporary eyes as a period of weird combinations: one of strikes and power cuts and struggling economies, all to the uplifting, hi-tech beat of *Star Wars* (1977) and disco. Understanding this weird mixture is nevertheless invaluable, mainly in our efforts to make sense of the mixed-up collage style that underpins Pegg and Wright's collaborative work, as well as some of their specific reference points, but also in recognising how the context of *Hot Fuzz*'s production and release are very specific to the beginning of the twenty-first century.

The comparison with Britpop actually has an added significance in the case of *Hot Fuzz*. It's worth noting how the traditions of British pop music, since its heyday in the 1960s, have revolved around the meeting of rock and roll and what we might call a British idiom. Bands like The Beatles and The Kinks (one of whose songs appears in *Hot Fuzz*), who would influence many of the Britpop groups, were particularly adept at infusing essentially American music forms with local colour, language and themes. Exactly how a film like *Hot Fuzz* deals with and incorporates the influence of American cinema is one of the most interesting and also important concerns of this book.

If we need a reminder of why this is, take note of the first thing we see when we sit down to watch *Hot Fuzz*: the Universal Pictures logo. In a book that will focus largely on the specific sense of *British* identity explored in the film, it is significant that our entry point should be one of the iconic signs in American film and television production. If you've never noticed this before, you either need to pay more attention, or at least make the effort to watch films from the beginning. Indeed, studying modern movies seriously, which involves looking at where they come from and how, requires us to look at opening credits with the same attention we might otherwise devote to traditional film studies subjects like narrative structure or *mise-en-scène*. If, equally, you're reading this book expecting a no-holds-barred celebration of young British movie-makers putting Hollywood in its place, accept my apologies once again, but this isn't quite the case with *Hot Fuzz*. If this isn't what you expected, I guess I have some explaining to do. The rest of the book will hopefully do just this.

The first chapter of this book, then, will locate *Hot Fuzz* within the contexts of early twenty-first century British cinema, and in particular, with regard to the production strategies and brand identity of Working Title, the film's producers. I will highlight the way that many of Working Title's most successful productions (*Notting Hill* [1999], *Bridget Jones's Diary* [2001], *Love Actually* [2003]), while often seen as 'typically British' in their tone and settings, are in reality very carefully constructed in their representation of British place and character. This, I suggest, is key to Working Title's success both domestically and globally, and it is an important indication of the way sustaining successful British cinema frequently means negotiating the economic demands of the global cinematic market. Nevertheless, while the Working Title context is an important one for understanding *Hot Fuzz*, I will argue that the latter film is actually more subtle than some of its Working Title predecessors in dealing with the British-Hollywood relationship.

Chapter two will take a detailed look at *Hot Fuzz*'s use of parody, particularly its manipulation of Hollywood action movie tropes. As I will show, uncritical discussions of parody in British film contexts, and with specific reference to *Hot Fuzz*, underestimate the ambiguous relationship of parody film to its 'targets'. Looking in detail at the film's style through chosen scenes, this chapter will identify what constitutes parody in this instance, given that much of the cinematic style of *Hot Fuzz* owes a debt to, rather than subverts, the Hollywood action movie. Looking closely at what the film really does with other films and television shows proves more revealing (and for me, much more interesting) than simply ticking off a list of reference points: a game which, fun as it may be, doesn't tell us a great deal about the film's, and consequently our, relationship to these same references.

Developing the discussion on parody in chapter two, the next chapter considers to what extent we may identify *Hot Fuzz* as an example of British national cinema. Looking in detail at some of the recent debates around national cinemas – do we define them in terms of the films we make, or the films we actually watch? Is national cinema a 'type' of film, or simply the films people prefer to see? Is the health of a national cinema related to the quantity of its income, or the quality of its output? – I argue that *Hot Fuzz* is positioned firmly at the centre of these discussions. As I suggest, *Hot Fuzz*'s use of relocated genre parody means that it addresses its audience in multiple but mutually reconcilable ways: as a 'Hollywood' movie that isn't quite Hollywood, and as a 'British' movie that acknowledges the possible limitations of 'British cinema' as a concept. I will also identify the ways in which *Hot Fuzz* references earlier examples of British television and cinema within its parodic references. As I discuss, the film makes significant narrative use of these inter-texts in ways that complicate the supposed direction of *Hot Fuzz*'s parody towards American cinema. I conclude then that part of *Hot Fuzz*'s appeal is the way it brings into focus various points of discussion about British cinema in the early twenty-first century, as well as offering an entertaining and economically viable response to these debates.

Chapter four will look more closely at the film's co-writer and star, Simon Pegg. As I argue here, *Hot Fuzz*, building on his previous performances in *Shaun of the Dead* and *Spaced*, allows Pegg to construct a particular kind of British movie star persona; one based largely on the identification of Pegg as a very untypical star. But I also draw on the earlier work on parody to argue that, both in *Hot Fuzz* and its predecessors, Pegg constructs a type of star persona around his own self-depiction as a fan, and through the practices of recognition and relocation inherent to parody film. Pegg's appeal, in other words, involves his own positioning as a fan, play-acting fanboy fantasies; fantasies which (certain) viewers may share and identify with. I therefore locate Pegg's star presence in *Hot Fuzz* both within the terms of millennial British masculinity, onscreen and off, but also in light of contemporary media theory (notably, Henry Jenkins' work on fans and 'participatory culture') that rethinks the cultural status of fans and their relationship to media texts.

The final chapter looks at some of the afterlives of *Hot Fuzz*, partly in terms of films that followed it, but particularly in terms of the fortunes of its main star, Pegg, and his collaborator Edgar Wright. As I will discuss, Pegg's seemingly improbable transition to (kind-of) Hollywood star, through his appearances in the *Mission: Impossible* and *Star Trek* franchises, has both helped maintain but also undermine his 'fan-star' persona. *Paul* (2010), in which Pegg starred and again co-wrote (this time with Nick Frost), while sharing points of similarity with *Hot Fuzz*, indicated a more 'mainstream' take on the earlier film's genre parody that suggested closer affinities to Hollywood. I will then look briefly at Wright's *Scott Pilgrim vs. The World*, and also *Attack the Block* (2011), a film produced by Wright, and one often discussed with reference to his earlier work. I then go on to look in more detail at Wright and Pegg's long-awaited *The World's End*. Casting a critical eye over these other films, as I will show, helps us to see a bit more clearly what gives *Hot Fuzz* its particular character, often through its difference to those other films that are supposedly its close relations.

A last point before we move on. If I don't spend much time in this book discussing some of the circumstances around *Hot Fuzz*'s production, this is largely because of space. But it's also because much of this is documented elsewhere. The internet has, in its serenely democratic way, made the job of the toiling film historian at once much easier and also largely redundant, given that so much information is widely available at the click of a mouse. You can also find plenty of shooting anecdotes and invaluable information on the film's technical side on the audio commentary on most DVD or Blu-ray versions of the film, if you have access to them: this is an invaluable resource for anyone studying the film closely, but because of its accessibility I won't refer to it here in much detail. Nor, as you should have realised by now, will I be reeling off an encyclopaedic list of *Hot Fuzz*'s various film and television references. Such things are again available on the internet, but in any case, as this introduction has hopefully made clear, what is most interesting about the film, or at least what lies beyond anecdotal discussion about the where and the who and the how of its production, is the question of what it *means*: its significance as a 'British film' about Britain in the early twenty-first century.

And finally, in case you're curious to know, while I will of course be looking in detail at numerous sequences, I won't be giving a scene-by-scene breakdown of everything that happens in *Hot Fuzz*. I'm assuming that, if you're reading this book, it's either because you've seen the film, or you haven't seen it but are planning to. Those of you who've seen the film won't need to know the plot; and I'm assuming those who haven't seen the film yet won't want to know it (be warned, though, that this book does contain spoilers, but then... well, you knew the risks when you picked it up). Whoever you are, if you're reading this I'm hoping it's because you find *Hot Fuzz* as entertaining, but also as interesting, as I do, and maybe – as I did when I first saw the film in 2007 – you got the urge to look at it even more closely, to try and work out what makes it tick. Sit back, then, lean forward, lie down: whatever. As Danny Butterman says, remote control in his hand, a copy of *Bad Boys II* ready to spin: 'This is about to go *off!*'

Footnotes

1. Wright's directorial debut is strictly speaking his very low-budget 1995 film *A Fistful of Fingers*, a parodic take on the western, filmed and set in Somerset.

2. See for example Manohla Dargis, '*Hot Fuzz*', *New York Times*, 20 April 2007; Chris Tookey, 'It aims. It fires. And yet somehow it misses', *Mail Online*, 20 February 2007.

3. Peter Bradshaw, '*Hot Fuzz*', *Guardian*, 16 February 2007.

4. See Dan Harries, 'Film Parody and the Resuscitation of Genre', in Steve Neale (ed.), *Genre and Contemporary Hollywood* (London: BFI, 2002), pp.281-293.

5. Richard Dyer, *Pastiche* (London and New York: Routledge, 2007), p.47.

6. Ernest Mathijs and Jamie Sexton, *Cult Cinema* (Chichester: Wiley-Blackwell, 2011), p.225.

7. Bradshaw, *op cit.*

One: Sandford, Hollywood: *Hot Fuzz* and the Business of British Cinema

From one point of view, the names and logos that appear at the start of a film have little relevance to the film itself. Logos like that of Universal's turning Earth, the Warner Bros. shield or the Paramount summit might be as familiar to us as chocolate bar wrappers, but like the latter, have little bearing on our enjoyment of the product. Even this analogy, in fact, has shortcomings: we need to at least to be able to recognise a packet of M&Ms if that's what we want to snack on, but I'm not sure anyone ever got the wrong movie because they couldn't tell their MGM from their RKO.

Do labels matter? Well for one thing, a logo, like a chocolate bar wrapper, is something you have to get through before you reach the main event, but it can also be part of this event itself. Perhaps it explains why I wound up talking about films for a living, but I've always been struck by the power of logos, and Hollywood ones in particular, to impact upon the start of a movie, to the extent that it becomes indivisible from the movie itself. *Star Wars* did this brilliantly, making the extended music over the 20th Century Fox searchlight image blend into the opening blast of the film's score – to the extent that I can rarely see the Fox opener anywhere without imagining John Williams' stirring music following it. A few years later, at the beginning of *Raiders of the Lost Ark* (1981), Steven Spielberg dissolved from the Paramount logo to a mountain within the world of the film's South American opening, thus incorporating classical Hollywood iconography into his playful homage to movies of the past. We might also think about the way the Warner Bros. 'WB' becomes more and more prominent (especially with the use of 3D) in the *Harry Potter* series, as intricate opening shots fly through the letters, in much the same way George Lucas's X-Wing fighters once ducked and dived through the Death Star.

'Studios' like Fox, Paramount and Warner Bros. aren't really studios anymore: even when Spielberg and Lucas were making these films decades ago, the Hollywood studios had ceased being definable locations of film production, and had become more a cluster of businesses with the capital to invest in film production. Films like *Star Wars* and *Raiders of the Lost Ark* may relish their continuity with old Hollywood history, but by making their corporate logos so prominent they are also making their sources of financing visible and celebrated.

We might not be that bothered by the logo for a Hollywood studio at the beginning of *Hot Fuzz*; we might, in fact, not even notice it at all. Its presence nevertheless raises significant questions about how we understand the film, especially in light of what we discussed in the introduction in terms of 'locating' the film. If we identify the Universal image for what it has traditionally represented – American film and (since the 1960s) American television – but see no discontinuity between it and *Hot Fuzz*, it can mean two things: either we no longer recognise the Universal logo as being attached exclusively to Hollywood (and the 'Universal' company is therefore living up to its name); or else, we take *Hot Fuzz* as a 'Hollywood' movie, or at least a film whose location is hardly of consequence. As we'll see, there is something in both of these readings. Alternatively, we might fail to acknowledge or even recognise the significance of the Universal symbol, but nonetheless persist in the conviction that *Hot Fuzz* is a resolutely 'British' piece of work. This, I will suggest, also contains grains of truth, but as a general conception around the film it is problematically limited, mainly because it avoids seeing or working out how films come to be made, why, and by whom.

Working Title's global Britain

As I noted earlier, *Hot Fuzz* can be located within a cycle of very successful films all produced by the British company Working Title. Working Title started out in the 1980s with very political dramas such as *My Beautiful Launderette* (1985), but became identified with a different type of product in subsequent decades. A quick survey of Working Title's most commercially popular films since the mid-1990s gives an indication of their economic but also cultural importance, as well as identifying the company as almost a brand of British filmmaking in itself. Starting with the unprecedented international success of *Four Weddings and a Funeral* (1994), the appeal of which to US audiences helped shape much of Working Title's later output, the company went on to finance a range of films including *Bean* (1997), *Notting Hill*, *Bridget Jones's Diary*, *About a Boy* (2002), *Love Actually*, *Johnny English* (2003), *Shaun of the Dead* and the previously-mentioned *Mr Bean's Holiday*. You don't need prodigious analytical skills to identify here the common threads that bind these films within what we might call the Working Title identity: the presence of very

'English' comic stars (Hugh Grant, Colin Firth, Rowan Atkinson), the use of identifiable and attractive English locations, a focus on the middle- and upper-middle classes, and an emphasis (especially in Grant's case) on genial and apparently irresistible English twits – or, in Atkinson's case, a celebration of English buffoons. Added to this is the dominance of the romantic comedy as the main genre of choice, especially in the hands of screenwriter Richard Curtis, and an interest in using American female stars (Andie McDowell, Julia Roberts, Renée Zellweger) as transatlantic counterpoints to the English male leads.

These films provide various, frequently illuminating representations of how England might see itself, or want to see itself, around the turn of the millennium, and the use of American stars and characters as romantic or dramatic foils is often a means of exploring Britain's evolving relationship with the rest of the world, and America especially.[8] We cannot properly understand these films, though, without also recognising that their international commercial success owed much to Working Title's business associations, first with the European media corporation Polygram,[9] and at the end of the 1990s, with Universal, itself a bigger shark in the same conglomerate that also, now, owned Polygram. After this point, Working Title enjoyed a distribution deal with Universal: in other words, Universal would cover the considerable expense of getting the films put on worldwide (something that entirely 'local' productions do not have the financial clout to achieve, hoping at best for the generation of good critical response and word-of-mouth). This partly accounts for the significant international success of these British productions. It also explains the logo at the start of *Hot Fuzz*.

The important point here is that 'Englishness' in these films is not some quality discerned transparently through these films' often very pretty windows-onto-the-world. Writers on film sometimes talk uncritically about the way films 'reflect' social realities, as if the movie screen were some form of unproblematic mirror for what is going on outside. In actual fact the idea of film as a mirror is not a bad analogy, as what we actually see in a mirror is not the real thing, but a version of it – and to some extent the version we want to see. In the case of the Working Title movies, we should also bear in mind that they are partly conceived as global products; versions of English location and character for an international audience. As film historian Andrew Higson argues,

Englishness is not an accidental or natural quality of these films: rather, it is itself the 'niche brand' that these films 'were conceived as vehicles for selling... in the international marketplace'.[10]

What for me makes *Hot Fuzz* an interesting film in this regard is that it does not try to hide either its resources or its influences. In many respects, like *Shaun of the Dead*, *Hot Fuzz* is in keeping with the Working Title brand: it makes use of recognisably English locations (here, Edgar Wright's home town of Wells standing in for the fictional Sandford), features a quirky English star (Pegg) and gets comic mileage out its very local contexts, with the film's action spilling out onto its church fetes, its market squares and even its model village. If we can assume that these characteristics helped the film to 'sell Englishness' as an international cinematic commodity, it is nevertheless worth noting that it does it in a slightly different way from the romantic comedies that have largely defined Working Title's output. Whether or not anyone really thinks films such as *Notting Hill* or *Bridget Jones's Diary* represent a place where people actually live, or that it still snows in central London, the films' narratives invite viewers to see their protagonists as *seemingly* real, in a film world that at least feels like it *might* exist. This is partly because the England of the Working Title rom-com is such a careful blend of beautiful but 'ordinary' characters, with settings that combine artifice and quirky urban detail, and stories that we can just about relate to, all combining to create a film world we can *sort of* recognise, and even might like to live in. Like many fiction films, needless to say, they are inherently contradictory, asking us to accept the proposition that Hugh Grant is a regular 'bloke', or to entertain the idea that the Texan movie star Renée Zelwegger in *Bridget Jones's Diary* is some kind of neurotic English everywoman.

By the time, eighty minutes into *Hot Fuzz*, Pegg's Police Sergeant rides into town on a white horse, an avenging Angel with two shotguns for wings [Fig 3], any thin veneer of realism, or what is often called 'verisimilitude' (literally 'real-seeming'), is well and truly blown away. In truth, though, the film has from its very beginning made no serious claims to believability. We'll look in more detail at the issue of parody in the next chapter, and in particular, how it works through manipulating the film knowledge and experience of viewers. Suffice it to say, though, that *Hot Fuzz* assumes a level of familiarity with certain conventions of filmmaking, without which the film would quite possibly make little sense.

Fig 3.

In terms of this chapter's focus, what is important to note here is the way the contradictions that are held in check in films like *About a Boy* or *Love Actually* are specifically made the comic centre of *Hot Fuzz*.

Back to those opening titles, then. We might easily overlook the fact that, while *Hot Fuzz* begins with a visual image of the Universal logo, we do not hear it. As film theorist Michel Chion has remarked, the tendency to talk about film soundtracks as if they are somehow 'added on' to what we see underestimates the way that what we 'see' is really a combination of what we see *and hear* (the 20th Century Fox logo, which is both a visual and familiar musical image, is a case in point here). Great moments in post-silent era film are often evoked in visual terms, privileging what we can describe with our eyes, but for Chion this is only half the story. The film 'image' for Chion is never just something we look at: what we hear at the same time gives this visual component its full meaning.[11] In *Hot Fuzz*, when the Universal name begins to unwrap itself around the slowly spinning globe, rather than the strident musical refrain we often hear, we get instead a mix of recognisable police noises on the soundtrack. Interestingly, this soundtrack combines the wail of modern police sirens, firstly, with obviously older car sirens, and secondly, with the more obviously antiquated sound of a clanging bell. From the very beginning, then, the audio-visual image *Hot Fuzz* presents to us is an odd one; the contemporary, corporate weight of the Hollywood studio sign and the deliberately retro sounds of the police force.

This is an interesting mix because it captures from the outset what the film will do for the next two hours. If *Star Wars* and *Raiders of the Lost Ark* blended their titles fluidly into the celebratory spectacle of Hollywood film-making, *Hot Fuzz* invites us to reflect on the meaning of putting one thing alongside another ('juxtaposition', to use the term I introduced previously). As we'll see, in Hot Fuzz there are two sides to this. On the most obvious side, it is about the significance of putting Hollywood genre narratives in an English village setting. But less obviously, and I think just as interestingly, it is about representing the motifs of the English police drama, possibly evoked by the sounds that open the film, through the stylistic conventions of the Hollywood genre film (interestingly, the looping tones of the police sirens work quite nicely with the corresponding, and in fact similar, visual movements: first, the reeling Universal title and turning globe, followed by the self-drawing circles that form the Working Title company image [Figs 4 and 5]).

Fig 4.

Fig 5.

Playing with Britishness: the opening sequence

Working Title's commercial achievement, as already noted, has been to 'present a version of life in the United Kingdom that is tremendously popular globally, especially in America'.[12] That this is very much an appealing *idea* of the country should by now be fairly obvious, but what Hot Fuzz does is to emphasise this highly constructed idea of Englishness right from the start. Because it uses techniques of parody such as exaggeration, literalisation and incongruity (more of which in the next chapter), *Hot Fuzz* constantly draws attention to the film world it creates, especially as so much of this parody works by juxtaposing seemingly antithetical ideas of Hollywood genre and English culture. We might overlook the fact, though, that in this process it is not just Hollywood genre that seems out of place: the 'English' world it establishes as its setting is also made to seem odd and unlikely. (I'll return to this idea of how the film explores national space and culture in chapter three.)

It is above all the *conscious*, or what some theorists call 'self-reflexive' nature of parody – its tendency to 'think about' its own representations – that makes it an interesting mode for exploring identity. Because parody frequently plays with aspects of genre film style, or narrative conventions, it also engages, often in a critical way, with the way films make sense to us; even when, as we've touched on here, this 'sense' is paradoxical. *Hot Fuzz* acknowledges its relationship to Hollywood from its opening, both as a source of financing and as a generic and stylistic influence. But it is also interested in what this actually means for the film – how, in other words, do you do an English story that is also 'made in Hollywood'? And if 'England' is a selling point for the global (and especially American) audience, what happens to this idea once it is packaged into a globally exportable form – in other words, the 'Hollywood movie'?

The opening sequence of *Hot Fuzz* offers a striking example of this balancing act. At the end of a long, sustained shot, in which a figure, silhouetted against a glowing background of glass and polished floor, comes slowly into focus, we see Pegg's intensely unsmiling face [Fig 6]. As the actor's voiceover introduces his character as Police Constable Nicholas Angel, he thrusts a London Metropolitan Police ('Met') ID card into close-up, the photo on it an exact replica of Pegg's expression in the first shot (in reality, a digital compositing of the previous shot onto the ID card) [Fig 7].

This moment of comic duplication (a familiar technique of film parody) establishes from the off that *Hot Fuzz* is not going to take its representation too seriously: the effect of duplicating Angel's super-serious face works here to make seriousness seem silly. It is consistent with the rest of the film, though, that this first shot carries with it a bold

Fig 6.

Fig 7.

sense of conviction and style that is not totally undermined by this initial instance of parodic play. The length of the opening shot, the dramatic nature of its composition, the purposeful intensity of Angel's approach to camera, all work to counterbalance the moment of duplication: while we may laugh at the repeated image of Pegg's face, then, it is – here as elsewhere – entirely in keeping with Angel's determined character, and overall, the film's insistence on playing things 'for real' even when the setting clearly suggests this is not possible.

As we see in the subsequent montage sequence, which rapidly narrates Angel's Met career to date, cataloguing his remarkable achievements, the film's style maintains a similar pitch which does not waver, even when the thing it depicts does not seem to match the intensity with which it is represented. So it is that a shot of Angel stopping his speeding police car in a screeching handbrake turn, cutting to an extreme close-up of Pegg turning intensely to camera, is followed by an almost identical sequence from the other angle – the difference being that Angel is now on a mountain bike wearing lycra shorts, and the extreme close-up has a helmeted Pegg staring manically through cycling goggles [Fig

8]. Naturally, the intended joke here is that 'advanced cycling' does not have the same edge, besides conjuring up long-held traditional images of British policemen on bicycles. But its humour stems mainly from the execution: the fact that all Angel's actions are conveyed with the same level of intense conviction, to the extent that performing a skidding stop on a mountain bike has the feel of heroic dynamism.

Fig 8.
'Advanced
cycling'

That we should get this sense at all from the initial sequence is entirely down to style. Wright is drawing on a range of aesthetic devices that, even if we do not explicitly register them in our everyday film viewing experience, are the stuff that make many recent Hollywood movies tick. Most obvious here is the speed and manner of the editing, characteristic of what David Bordwell has called the 'intensified continuity' style of Hollywood and its global imitators.[13] In the modern blockbuster film, for example, we rarely see the measured and economical movement from shot to shot, from camera spot to camera spot, and from character to character, that are the hallmarks of Hollywood films during its 'classical' period of the 1930s to the 1950s. Modern movies frequently feel the need to move the camera around where once a fixed shot would do, to ramp up or slow down film speed, and to find as many ways as possible of cutting action up into fragments or bursts of information – even to the extent where 'continuity', the illusion of a film's edited sequence happening in real, uninterrupted time, falls apart.

The opening sequence from *Hot Fuzz* is almost an experiment in using the full resources of intensified continuity. Notice how Wright frequently 'flashes' the image; an effect created to give the appearance of brief over-exposure, and with it a sudden pulse of light. Or when, cutting between the shots of Angel in field-work training and in riot mode, he uses quickly varying speeds and super-imposed shots; techniques which detract from our ability to properly make sense of what we see, but which notionally increase (or in Bordwell's terms, 'intensify') the impact of the image. Similarly, a fixed camera is rarely employed when a moving one can't be used instead. So it is that we get forward tracking shots to close-up in the least dramatic of contexts: here, as Angel, sitting at a school desk, finishes as exam with a confident click of his ball-point pen.

Consider as well the inventive ways the film moves between different shots, even within this short sequence. In keeping with Bordwell's observation that modern filmmakers look to 'create a percussive burst of images',[14] Wright marks the cuts between shots with specific actions, using camera flashes, the button of a slide-show remote, the clicking of the aforementioned pen [Figs 9 and 10], or the bell of a chess clock being pressed.

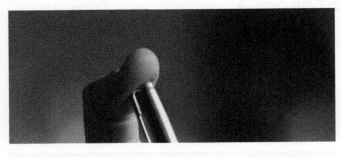

Fig 9. A thumb presses a pen...

Fig 10. ... detonating the flash of a camera bulb

The sequence also makes good use of the movement of one shot into the next: hence, at one point, Angel turns a corner in the police station, our sight momentarily blocked by part of the building, at which point the shot shifts to Angel, now armed and armoured, at the foot of a staircase, but moving in the same direction as in the previous shot. Both here and later in the film, Wright is keen to 'refresh' the screen through a characteristic use of the 'wipe-by cut': a technique in which, typically, a blurred foreground object 'wipes' across the screen, revealing an adjusted shot (sometimes a different framing of the same shot, or even a different location or character) in place of the old one. Elsewhere in this sequence, we see the wipe-by cut used to illustrate the different community figures Angel engages with, as a symmetrical shot of Pegg in the middle of two elderly ladies cuts to the same composition, but now with an Asian couple and the backdrop of London's Chinatown. At the end of the sequence, meanwhile, Wright has a shot from behind of Angel in the police station, walking towards the door which, it turns out, is where his subsequent promotion to (country) sergeant will take place. Rather than run the shot in an unbroken sequence, Wright uses two wipe-bys, subtly reframing the following shot and making Angel slightly bigger in each one; until finally, in close-up, he reaches and knocks on the door.

As with the shot of the mountain bike, it's the movement between dynamism and the mundane – or rather, the mundane *as dynamic* – that makes this sequence work, and what makes it a little more than just a bravura statement of intent on the part of the filmmakers. The stylistic flourishes are constantly balanced by the setting and design, with the police training college looking more like an English secondary school (a point further reinforced by the little shorts and white polo shirts Angel and the other trainees wear). In the world of *Hot Fuzz* a multiple-choice exam, like police admin, is edited to look like an action sequence; giving directions to elderly couples becomes exciting and kinetic. Regular police work, the frequently televisual stuff of plodding 'bobbies on the beat', looks like the most thrilling job in the world.

It seems off-target though to assume that the film is mocking its main character, or the Metropolitan Police Force. The clever use of the 1982 Adam Ant hit 'Goody Two Shoes' in the soundtrack seems to be having a bit of fun at Angel's expense; we might also note that Angel's number, as seen on his shoulder, is 777, the godly alternative to Satan's 666. But the sequence also celebrates Angel's work in its stylistic, kinetic verve. Equally, given the confident and inventive way the sequence embraces the aesthetics of contemporary Hollywood movies, it is hard in this instance to suggest that the latter are the target of any parodic criticism. As I've already suggested, mockery seems too strong a word to apply here. What the sequence does is establish a set of apparent cultural oppositions, an unexpected mix of content and context. Linda Hutcheon, a theorist who established many of the key debates around parody back in the 1980s, describes this mixing as 'trans-contextualization', a form of 'repetition with difference':[15] the relocation of a set of stylistic conventions to another, unexpected and unfamiliar place. For Hutcheon, one of the aims of this process is to show how styles, and especially styles associated with genres, are made to seem strange when taken away from their usual associations: in the case, say, of the action movie, such associations could include particular stars and types of location. Parody often works in this way to show how genres and different settings are irreconcilable or ridiculous.

Where's the joke?

But – and it's a big but – if the mix in *Hot Fuzz* seems incongruous, it begs the question why this should be so. In other words, what makes one concept of cinema 'Hollywood' and the other 'British'? Is the idea of English police admin as action movie so laughable, and if so, why? Like the rest of the film, the opening of *Hot Fuzz* throws a variety of things into its mix without necessarily indicating where one thing stands in relation to another. As I'll explore in the next two chapters, one of the film's significant achievements is to complicate the presumed boundaries between so-called Hollywood and national cinematic styles, with important implications for how we understand both 'American' and 'British' cinema in the twenty-first century.

To return finally to the question I asked at the beginning of the chapter: does it matter what logo we see at the beginning of a film, and does it matter where the film comes from? My discussion here has suggested that it does, in both cases. This is because, as viewers, we may identify with films in certain ways that overlook their own origins or the circumstances in which they were made. Understanding these circumstances enables us to have a realistic view of the way films get made and screened in the twenty-first century, and also encourages us to recognise the limitations of putting films into neat, sometimes oppositional boxes ('British' and 'Hollywood' cinema, say). But it also, from another perspective, asks us to think about whether contemporary movies are really 'all the same', and what space there is for cultural and national difference in a marketplace that is both global and consistently dominated by Hollywood.

As I've considered, with relation to the recent success of Working Title's range of comedies, *Hot Fuzz* is quite consistent with their tendency to produce versions of Englishness for global audiences. The fact that Working Title rom-coms consistently make the Anglo-American relationship central to their romance plots – or, in *Love Actually*, the more edgy relationship between the British Prime Minister and the US President[16] – indicates that these films rarely offer an unreflective chocolate-box Britain for the rest of the world (their own domestic audience, of course, remains a key part of the company's success). Notably, though, what is less frequently explored or questioned in these films is the centrality of the romantic comedy form itself: a type of story structure that, though arguably invented by Shakespeare in plays like *Much Ado About Nothing*, was perfected by Hollywood in the 1930s and has been a staple of its output ever since. *Hot Fuzz* is no less aware of the significance of Hollywood film form as a means of extending British cinema production's global reach. Where films like *Notting Hill* explore the possible tensions between English and American culture through their stories and characters, though, *Hot Fuzz*, whose only Americans appear on television screens, explores this at the level of style and its relationship to content. It does this, as we've established, through parody: the next chapter will look at this in more detail.

Footnotes

8.   See John Fitzgerald, *Studying British Cinema 1999-2009* (Leighton Buzzard: Auteur, 2010), pp.48-52.

9.   See Andrew Higson, *Film England: Culturally English Filmmaking since the 1990s* (London and New York: I.B. Tauris, 2011), p.17.

10. Higson, *op cit.*, p.30.

11. Michel Chion, *Audio-Vision: Sound on Screen* (New York: Columbia University Press, 1994).

12. Fitzgerald, *op cit.*, p.48.

13. David Bordwell, *The Way Hollywood Tells It: Story and Style in Modern Movies* (Berkeley: University of California Press, 2006), pp.121-138.

14. Bordwell, *op cit.*, p.123.

15. Linda Hutcheon, *A Theory of Parody: The Teachings of Twentieth-Century Art Forms* (New York: Methuen, 1985), p.32.

16. Fitzgerald, *op cit.*, p.48.

Two: The Shit Just Got Real: *Hot Fuzz* and the Uses of Parody

As we saw when looking in detail at *Hot Fuzz*'s opening sequence, much of the film's comedy comes from the way it plays with, and frequently deviates from, expectation. The shot of Pegg at the beginning of the film, as I've already suggested, is funny in its use of duplication. It might partly be amusing because our prior expectations of Simon Pegg, and a film with him in it, mean we are predisposed not to take him seriously. But above all, the humour here is again based around surprise and rhythm, the absolutely identical photographic image being at once improbable and ridiculous.

Probably my favourite piece of comic business in *Hot Fuzz* is the bit where Angel, newly promoted to his position as Sergeant, goes to speak to his estranged girlfriend, the enigmatic Janine. Janine works as part of a police forensics team, and when Nicholas finds her she is going over a crime scene with her similarly masked and plastic-suited colleagues. We see Angel calling Janine from the other side of a window, looking in, saying they need to talk. Subsequently, from the interior of the building, we see Angel enter and approach the nearest masked figure. 'Janine, I've been transferred, I'm moving away for a while,' he says. 'I'm not Janine,' a man's voice replies [Fig 11]. Angel turns round and says the exact same words to another figure, who indeed turns out to be Janine, and the scene continues [Fig 12].

Pegg's beautifully straight playing is part of what makes this sequence work (admittedly, much better on screen than on the page): note the way his reaction and repeated line delivery register not a flicker of surprise or adjustment, allowing the timing and the situation to speak for itself. There's humour here in terms of the absurdity, of course, in trying to speak intimately to specific individuals in a room full of identical people (I'll return to this scene briefly at a later point). But the scene works equally through the way it sets up a fairly standard expectation for the narrative (Nicholas enters and speaks to Janine) only to flip these expectations so bluntly, so absurdly.

I've tried to indicate in these brief analyses how much the humour of films like *Hot Fuzz* (or indeed any film) is rarely 'simply funny', but works

Fig 11.

Fig 12.

through a kind of dialogue with the viewer: one between the film and the viewer's familiarity with cinema and its conventions. The film is funny in this way by not doing what we might, in some part of our minds, expect it to do. The surprise, the deviation from expectation, as in many of the best jokes, is what makes us laugh. But this laughter comes largely from our knowledge of what the film is deviating from, whether this is a very specific prior text (another film, for example) or more simply the familiar conventions of films and genres.

This idea of playing with and deviating from the motifs of cinema, and what we might call film's 'language', is central to our understanding of parody, which is the main focus of this chapter. As we'll see, *Hot Fuzz* is adept at manipulating cinematic conventions to comic effect, and it is worth looking in some detail at how it achieves this. One of my aims is to think very specifically about what *Hot Fuzz* actually *does* as a film. As I touched upon earlier, one of the (for me) less interesting ways to view this film is as a series of pop-cultural reference points or 'homages'. One of the limitations in viewing a film in this way is that it turns into an exercise in demonstrating the viewer's cultural knowledge, but not much else.

More to the point, it does not really explain *Hot Fuzz*'s quality and appeal. It's actually not very difficult to reference films and television shows in a film. Anyone with the right software can paste a film together this way and stick it on YouTube. Whether it would be any good or not, though, would entirely depend upon the skill and ingenuity with which such references were integrated within the new text made up of them. This is why the study of a film type such as parody, which works explicitly through such references, requires as equally close attention to the details of film style as any other kind of movie.

It's also worth noting that, in *Hot Fuzz*, parody is not always so easy to pin down. As Henry K. Miller remarks in a perceptive review, *Hot Fuzz* is quite different from *Spaced*, and to some extent from *Shaun of the Dead*, in making its most obvious reference point – *Bad Boys II* – a film that many fans of Pegg and Wright's work would not, unless perhaps ironically, accept within the ranks of 'cool' film and television texts.[17] I personally find *Hot Fuzz*'s use of supposedly 'bad' texts like *Bad Boys II* both interesting and revealing, as we'll see. But this makes it very different from *Spaced*, which as Miller points out expected a significant amount of pop-cultural acumen on the part of its audience. The way that *Spaced* more or less demands that viewers 'get' the joke, with its plethora of references to *Star Wars* lore, *The Shining* (1980), *The Evil Dead* (1982), and a variety of television shows, from *The A-Team* (1983–7) to *The X-Files* (1993–2002) via *Grange Hill* (1978–2008), has in fact made it the subject of criticism from some scholars working on television comedy.[18] But a frequent problem in *Spaced* (which for the most part is, I think, a wonderfully innovative show) is less the quantity or nature of reference, than the sometimes rather self-satisfied way such references are incorporated without actually doing anything with them. The result is that we nod knowingly at such reference points, but then – unless having your pop-cultural ego flattered is sufficient – we ask of the show: 'So what?'

Hot Fuzz is much more interesting in its choices of convention to exploit, largely because they are neither quite so obvious nor quite so hip. The equally important question though, and one which I'll continue to explore in the chapter that follows, is the *meaning* of this parody. This might seem an over-elaborate question – isn't the comedy in *Hot Fuzz* just there to make us laugh? – but I think it's one we should ask. After all, if parody makes us laugh by manipulating or deviating from the conventions of cinema, it seems to imply a type of relationship or attitude towards these same conventions; or at least, it asks us by its own nature to think about these conventions. Until fairly recently, probably because of the incorrect assumption that comic texts can't be the source of serious consideration, parody films have not received a huge amount of critical attention or close analysis. Lately, though, writers on film have begun to see parody as an often complex and highly significant form of cinema, especially in the contexts of the early twenty-first century.

The language of parody

I'm sure most of us have an intuitive sense of what parody is: in the same way that we recognise a thriller or a rom-com, we tend to know what parody is when we see it, even if we can't immediately identify what makes it so. As it turns out, something as 'obvious' and 'light' as parody film – there may be many people who find *Airplane!* or *The Naked Gun* either hilarious or boring, though few I suspect would find them 'challenging' – proves very difficult to pin down in simple terms. Arguably the best, most thorough work on parody (though mainly restricted to the US context) is Dan Harries' *Film Parody*. In his first chapter, Harries offers a working definition for his chosen subject of study:

> I define parody as the process of recontextualizing a target or source text through the transformation of its textual (and contextual) elements... This conversion – through the resulting oscillation between similarity to and difference from the target – creates a level of ironic incongruity with an inevitable satiric impulse.[19]

Someone seeing this definition out of context might be surprised to find that it referred to a film like *Spaceballs* (1987). But Harries' admittedly very dense outline for a definition highlights the elaborate and often complex ways we make sense of these otherwise obvious or even 'silly' films. This is because parody, even at its most crude – and I'm probably not alone in thinking that *Spaceballs* is a very, very bad film – involves the identification of various 'inter-texts', and the recognition of how these various texts are reworked or relocated in the new text represented by the parody film.

While, like its predecessors *Spaced* and *Shaun of the Dead*, *Hot Fuzz* contains many allusions to other films, *Hot Fuzz* works mainly through its use of the broader, generic frameworks through which we view cinema. This is by definition quite vague, though it's these same frameworks of viewing that enable us to quickly identify genres, or know where and when films have come from, without being able to put our fingers on how. But it's also this intuitive sense of recognition that enables us to make sense of films *in general*. Our ability to comprehend the sequence of fragmented images that make up a film, for us to follow this as if it were a piece of 'real life', unfolding in real time before our eyes, is not a skill we are born with: rather it is one we acquire through experience of watching other films. This makes *all* movies 'inter-textual' to some extent. And this is also how we can talk about film as a kind of language: sequences of film make sense to us in a similar way to sentences and combinations of sentences.

When this language plays out in a way based on our expectations, it feels natural. When our expectations are not met, the result is either confusion or, in the case of jokes, amusement. In *Hot Fuzz*, Angel chases a shell-suited biscuit thief through the back-alleys of Sandford, turns a corner and comes to an abrupt halt. We see him looking angrily past the camera. 'You *mothers!*' he curses [Fig 13]. At which point, the reverse shot reveals who Angel is addressing: a group of young mums with pushchairs, blocking Angel's path [Fig 14].

This works first and foremost because it's a great pun, the tough, implied expletive quickly qualified by the revelation that these mothers are exactly what Angel is describing (Harries calls this technique 'literalization'). But it only really works because the concepts are so disparate; from the 'mother(fucker)s' implied within the generic contexts of a criminal chase, to the sunny mums we then see. But as is typical in Wright's films more generally, the real key here is the way the joke plays on the expectations of editing and the use of off-screen space. The sequence cues our expectations in one way – the anguished look off-screen, the anticipation of disappointment or confrontation, perhaps – only to surprise us with the opposite of these expectations.

As I've said, the pressing issue here is what all these games with generic expectation mean for us, in terms of our relationship, firstly, to *Hot Fuzz*,

Fig 13.

Fig 14.

and secondly, to the type of cinema being referenced. As I'll go on to explore in more detail in the next chapter, this is an important question because it relates to the ways we might identify with Wright and Pegg's film, but also – importantly – with the cinema that is in theory the 'target' of its parody. We therefore need to think a bit not just about what parody is and how it works, but what kinds of attitudes are supposedly connoted by it.

Parody and/as criticism

The quote above from Harries identifies the way that parody has a 'satiric impulse'. Satire, as Geoff King has identified, is often confused with parody. There are grey areas between the two, but satire in itself always has a specific target in the 'institutions of the real world', especially 'social and political' areas of concern.[20] The main traditions of satire in both Britain and the US, for example, in television shows such as *Spitting Image* (1984–96), *Have I Got News For You* (1990–) and *The Daily Show* (1996–), or websites like *The Onion*, focus principally on the politics, current affairs and celebrity culture that consistently fill our media. Satire like this may use parody as a technique; reworking the style and format of newspaper journalism, for example, or the characteristics of political broadcasting. But parody in itself need not have 'real world' aims; rather, its target tends to be 'formal or aesthetic'.[21]

King nevertheless points out, correctly, that parodying 'formal or aesthetic' aspects of films, genres, or even the familiar language of cinema itself, is rarely without 'social or political implications'.[22] This makes sense if we take the view that Hollywood and its cinematic products are themselves an 'institution' whose effects are both social and political. From this perspective, Hollywood products such as action movies are mass-entertainment machines designed to sell formulae and stereotypes for economic profit. They also communicate what critics call an 'ideology', a way of thinking or a belief system, which they commonly do by making this system of belief seem totally natural and inevitable. This is often achieved, so the theory suggests, by making the narrative of genre films appear to develop in a realistic and credible fashion, to the extent that we don't even notice what kind of values are being 'sold' to us by the predominantly US-centred capitalist enterprise that is Hollywood. This is part of the reason why action movies are often held in such low opinion by critics of film: not only, such critics suggest, are they too fast, too loud and too predictable, but they are frequently racist, sexist and uncritically flag-waving endorsements of the American way of life.

Harries consequently argues that one of parody's roles is to disrupt the 'norms' (the common expectations, in other words) of popular narrative film, with the aim that this 'normative disruption might somehow jar the spectator into questioning norms in general – taking a more critical stance toward "every day" normative assumptions'.[23] Parody is therefore directed at the 'system' of a genre or narrative film more broadly: those codes and structures that enable movies to 'make sense' to viewers. The process through which parody offers us at once 'similarity' with its target and 'difference' from it enables us to see how the target works, and in the process, to reflect upon it. Applying this to *Hot Fuzz*, the scenes described at the beginning of this chapter all provide slight variations on familiar conventions, but the deviations at work may be seen to satirise the 'natural' conventions that are their basis.

Elsewhere, we could argue, the ideologies of genre are more obviously targeted. Toward the end of the film, Nicholas and Danny look out from the supermarket office window [Fig 15] to see Simon Skinner, the supermarket owner and their chief suspect, making a getaway.

Nicholas to Danny: We need to get down there.
Danny: How?
Nicholas, looking down: Skip!

The next shot gives us a high-angle slow-motion shot of Angel leaping down into a waiting skip full of black rubbish bags [Fig 16].

Fig 15.

Fig 16.

This apparently throwaway gag is another example of the 'literalization' technique popular in parody texts, but it also uses forms of 'misdirection', in which one expected outcome deviates suddenly. Like the earlier 'mothers' joke, this is not just an agile little pun (at least for anyone who knows what a skip is): humour is also derived from the contexts and expectations of the genre. Angel's initial injunction to 'skip' is already bizarre, given how out of keeping it is with the very masculine connotations of the Hollywood action hero – not to mention the fact that it is a very ineffective way of chasing anyone. The revelation that this 'skip' is actually the object below makes Angel's sudden shift off-genre 'normal' again, but at the same time it highlights the ways action films often provide such ludicrously fortuitous get-outs for their protagonists – the softly-padded skip simply waiting, it seems, for the heroes to dive into, satisfying the spectacular demands of the action movie. Consequently, this parodic sequence 'disrupts' the masculine prowess implicitly celebrated in the action genre's 'system' of representation.

Unsurprisingly, some theorists have suggested that parody plays an important role in the way non-Hollywood cinemas relate to, and express their distinction from – or their criticism of – Hollywood genre cinema. James Leggott, in a recent book on contemporary British cinema, has made this point, arguing that Hot Fuzz employs a 'mocking' approach to the action genre. For Leggott, who makes a similar point regarding the use of the musical genre in The Full Monty (1997), the more low-budget and realist commitments of British cinema preclude a fuller and non-ironic engagement with these essentially Hollywood modes of filmmaking.[24] Leggott touches here upon the very significant issue of the expectations and horizons of filmmaking in Britain, and its relationship to Hollywood's dominant and economically overpowering cinematic muscle. I'll look at this in more detail later, but it's worth picking up for now on the assumption that Hot Fuzz 'mocks' its target texts or genres in this way. Does it necessarily follow that a parody always has a 'satirical' impulse? And if it doesn't, what exactly is it doing?

Hot Fuzz: 'parody without criticism'

As many theorists of parody have pointed out, parody need not be critical in the way it identifies and plays with other films, styles and genres. King summarises this neatly when he argues:

> Parody... can offer something of the best of all worlds. It offers the pleasure of standing back from familiar conventions, to see them for what they are, as constructs that are often ridiculous when extrapolated [that is, taken out of context] or otherwise subjected to closer examination. But it can also play positively on our familiarity with and continued enjoyment of the deployment of the same conventions.[25]

Wes Gehring has called these 'parodies of reaffirmation'; films which work to produce 'a fascinating tension between genre expectations... and a parody that is comic without deflating the characters involved'.[26] To illustrate his point, Gehring gives the very useful example of director John Landis's *An American Werewolf in London* (1981), which manages to be both a very contemporary, graphic horror film, and also a film that refers knowingly to horror cinema more broadly, with its jokey soundtrack (songs like 'Blue Moon' and 'Bad Moon Rising') and its supporting cast of British local yokels who seem to know the rules of the horror film better than its young American stars ('Keep off the moors!'). Pegg, who went on to work with Landis in 2008's *Burke and Hare*, cites *An American Werewolf in London* as a key influence.[27] What the latter film and Pegg's work clearly do share is the idea that you can allude knowingly, and playfully, to the rules of a genre without actually leaving the framework of that same genre. *Shaun of the Dead*, for example, constantly acknowledges and inverts its generic precedents. Its main comic premise, in fact – that the zombie invasion is barely noticed by its protagonists until it's almost too late – plays with our knowledge of the genre and its comic inversions in the film's narrative. But like *An American Werewolf in London* it's still a genre film full of visceral violence, emotion, and heroism (of sorts). Similarly, in some of the examples outlined above, we can see how the generic narrative structure of *Hot Fuzz* remains intact even as generic motifs are being parodied: Nicholas must still negotiate the 'mothers' who get in the way of his pursuit; the skip is a ridiculous and arbitrary plot convenience but it still enables the protagonists to execute a stunt and continue the chase – a stunt which, as I've shown above, is filmed with little difference from a 'straight' action movie.

I say 'straight' with deliberate caution, because it begs the question of whether the supposed targets of recent parody films are actually so serious in the first place. The logic of parody as a form of criticism or 'mockery' implies that its objects are worthy of such scorn, probably because they are ideologically incorrect and/or aesthetically bereft. But this may be going too far. From one logical point of view, our ability to identify and predict generic conventions is already an indication that genre films cannot exert their influence unconsciously, and that we are already watching them in a knowing way. Critics more favourable to the action genre have identified the way it is frequently very self-conscious about itself and its representations. As these films then generate franchises, and in turn loyal and knowledgeable fans, they are typically very knowing in their allusions to the earlier films and repeated motifs (note how often, for example, John McLane in the *Die Hard* films [1998–2013] comments on his unerring ability to find himself in similar situations). There is by definition a high degree of predictability built into such genre series, but a lot of the fun viewers experience in watching these films is expecting this, and often enjoying the variations on a familiar theme. We know that McLane will end up in his vest, but we can't say when or why; we know he will dispatch the bad guys with a clever bit of pay-off dialogue, but we don't know how or with what kind of line. The fact that such films work around conventional narrative structures is hardly the point. Most stories do: that's how their structures become conventional!

An example of *Hot Fuzz* showing this genre awareness is during the supermarket shoot-out, when Angel has finally (and rather unconvincingly) dispatched the giant trolley-boy 'Lurch' by spinning him into a freezer full of peas. Angel slides down the aisle, guns in each hand, and ends up crouched next to Danny, who is holding a shotgun:

Danny: Where's the trolley boy?

Nicholas: In the freezer.

Danny: Did you say 'cool off?'

Nicholas: No I didn't say anything...

Danny: Shame.

Nicholas: Well, there was the bit that you missed where I distracted him with the cuddly monkey, then I said 'play time's over' and I hit him in the head with the peace lily.

Danny: You're off the fucking chain!

There is again an ambivalent relationship to genre conventions here. The fact that the narrative effectively pauses here for a *discussion about* the use of quality pay-off lines holds up to comic scrutiny the similar ways many action movies, and the stars associated with them (Bruce Willis and Arnold Schwarzenegger, all the Bonds until Daniel Craig), feel the need, and have the time, to get in a suitably sardonic jibe at their usually dead opponent. If we enjoy this dialogue, though, it is probably because we warm to the way Nicholas, in his typically cerebral manner, *tries* to come up with the line and the right timing for it. But it is also possibly because we are aware of the convention from other films, and identify the way the convention is relocated to *Hot Fuzz*'s setting and characters.

Though there isn't really space for it here, we could give many other examples of the way genre series offer forms of repetition and variation, providing the different but compatible pleasures of familiarity and innovation (the *Indiana Jones* [1981–2008] and Bond [1962–] movies, other action franchises like *Lethal Weapon* [1987–98] or *The Expendables* [2010–]). Suffice it to say for now that the big-budget genre movie, whether we enjoy such films or not, is rarely as categorically 'bad' as some might have it. But if, as these last examples suggest, the targets of much film parody are *already parodying themselves*, what does this say about the place of modern parody film and its point in our film culture?

Harries' interesting take on this is that our contemporary viewing experience is one of 'ironic supersaturation': one in which almost *every* film is a potential source of ironic reflection and knowing appropriation, and where almost no film is really so serious it can't be the source of parodic fun. This explains the somewhat paradoxical state of affairs in which, especially since the 1970s, there are more and more parody films, but with less and less to actually critically say about the films they reference. As I've mentioned, and as both Harries and King point out, this is hardly surprising, as increasingly the intended viewers for both the parody series and its apparent target – for the *Scary Movie* films and the *Final Destination* (2000–11) franchise, for example – are one and the same: the youthful demographic that continue to make up the dominant audience for contemporary cinema. For Harries, many of the viewers for these films are simply not worried about the distinctions, or at least they enjoy them both the same – in an 'ironic' manner, perhaps – identifying and enjoying their different and shared generic characteristics.

As Harries says, he started to think about this when one of his students asked if *Airport*, the 1970 star-studded disaster movie, was based on *Airplane!* – the film that effectively buried the airline movie as a sub-genre ten years later.[28] Besides indicating that parody films like *Airplane!* are more often than not enjoyed without any specific knowledge of its main reference points, this story is very revealing about the ways parodies can actually teach us about how genre films work (Gehring uses the term 'creative criticism' to describe what parody films do).[29] The student commenting on *Airport* could obviously see the mechanics of the earlier movie already laid bare in *Airplane!*, to the extent that the 'target' and the 'parody' were no longer so obvious. Our familiarity with parody in contemporary culture, extending through films, DIY filmmaking on YouTube, and mainstream television shows such as *The Simpsons* (1989–) and *Family Guy* (1999–), is partly a cause of this textual awareness when it comes to watching film and television. But it is also an effect. Parody may inform us critically, but so common is it now that it begs the question who actually *needs* it anymore, given that everyone is a parodist, and the Emperor that is Hollywood is quite obviously – perhaps shamelessly – not wearing any clothes.

The implication for the study of *Hot Fuzz* in light of the Hollywood action movie is that, far from a problem to be criticised, the latter is simply something to be used and enjoyed. Relocating the familiar aspects of the genre to Sandford plays a role here, of course, because – to follow the logic of trans-contextualization – we can't take it seriously in this setting. But our familiarity and critical sense has perhaps already removed whatever nasty sting supposedly lurked in the genre film: what can't hurt us, then, can be a source of pleasure. This is not to let all action movies off the hook in a sweeping gesture. Just because we 'know what they are doing' does not necessarily forgive the often xenophobic, militaristic or misogynistic characteristics some such films (*Bad Boys II* being a case in point) display. But it *does* suggest that once we are able to separate a genre's style and motifs from its familiar contexts – American military veterans battling with terrorists, say, or free-wheeling cops targeting 'criminal' ethnic minorities – style becomes trappings that you can reuse to entirely different, and less politically awkward, effect.

Style as substance

A good example of this particular use of parody in *Hot Fuzz* is the point at which Nicholas and Danny leave the village square after the opening shootout sequence. As the Doctor lies on the ground clutching his foot, an arcing camera picks up the two protagonists, moving around them one way, and then the other. This is of course a direct use of the same technique used in the earlier quoted sequence from *Bad Boys II*, and has become a signature style for shooting many otherwise static talking scenes in modern Hollywood, turning dialogue into a dynamic moment.[30] Notably, though, there is no effort to make a joke out of this stylistic tick, nothing that would draw attention to the style in a way that would disrupt its normal meaning. Similarly, the series of shots that sees them entering the pub to attack the landlords, while indicating the highly constructed nature of action genre motifs, does not obviously seek to undermine this motif by doing anything different with its 'system' of representation. Here, Nicholas and Danny come surging through the open doorway in a lateral dive, both with guns blazing in either hand. In an elaborately edited stunt (there are over fifteen different shots in the fifteen-second sequence between them entering and hitting the floor), we see both the protagonists and their targets from a series of different angles and speeds, moving between close-ups and longer framings, and between slow motion and real time [Figs 17–19]. Each subsequent shot of Nicholas and Danny overlaps slightly with the previous one, increasing the effect of suspension that gives the stunt its impact, until finally the duo hit the ground and the sequence resumes at normal speed. This is both a type of stunt and mode of representing it (above all, the use of temporal overlapping) common in Hong Kong action cinema: we see a very similar sequence at several points, for example, in director John Woo's film *Hard Boiled* (1992), with Chow Yun-Fat doing the diving.

Once more, the reference is not really the point, as Hong Kong action cinema is probably obscure to many viewers in the UK or elsewhere, and the allusion is general and stylistic rather than specific to any film. The significant point is that the style is incorporated into *Hot Fuzz* in such a way that, even without any context for such a sequence, *it can be enjoyed for what it is*, rather than for what it supposedly parodies. Arguably, as in much of the film's action, there is pleasure in seeing the incongruous sight of Pegg and Frost going head-on through the range of great action genre moves; but there is again no obvious sense that this 'language' of action cinema is being undermined. Obviously artificial and unreal this type of action sequence is, within its generic terms the stunt plays out as normal, on the right side of generic verisimilitude. It is as 'cool' as it is potentially funny.

Fig 17.

Fig 18.

Fig 19.

Just Bolognese

But doesn't this perhaps let the amount of *violence* in the film go unremarked? It's interesting that some reviews in the British tabloid press picked up critically on the film's apparent celebration of movie gun culture:[31] a traditionally thorny issue in discussions around cinematic representation and its possible influence on viewers. Certainly *Hot Fuzz* gives ammunition (as it were) to the apologists for such types of film.

Hard Boiled in fact has one of the grisliest body-counts of any film I've seen, with its chorus of balletic, bullet-jiggled Cantonese crooks flying between spraying sub-machine guns. This is not the place for a debate on the ethics of cinematic violence, but we should note that *Hot Fuzz*'s status as a parody text goes some way to putting this in perspective.

A wonderful moment that illustrates this is in the supermarket showdown, when one of the 'Andys' (Sandford's two, formerly indifferent mustachioed detectives) is peering round a corner stacked with spaghetti sauce. A knife hurled from the men behind the meat counter shatters the bottles, spraying Andy's face with red goo. The other Andy screams in fury and raises his gun to fire. 'It's okay!' yells the first Andy across the aisle: 'It's just Bolognese!' [Fig 20].

Fig 20.

Aside from the obvious pleasure in hearing the generally very intense Paddy Considine say this line (listen to the marvelous way he draws out the last syllable), this line sums up what *Hot Fuzz* is actually doing. Yes: it's just Bolognese; just as the 'blood' Danny uses in his earlier fork trick, or that on Lurch's bald head, is just ketchup. But in action movies as a whole, this is all it ever is, or at least other synthetic variants on the real thing. The extremely vast majority of fans of action cinema – those who have a clear conception of the difference between fiction and reality – know this. And in any case *Hot Fuzz*, in which no one is actually killed by Nicholas and Danny's bullets, has already looked to forge a safe space of cinematic fun by being a parody to start with: a cinematic space where you can't really take anything too seriously. All that weaponry and action-movie posturing in *Hot Fuzz* shed little more than Dolmio. Which for my mind (and because I'm not a vampire, or a fan of real-life violence) is actually much tastier than real blood.

Footnotes

17. Henry K. Miller, 'Hot Fuzz', Sight & Sound 17.4 (2007), p.66.

18. Brett Mills, for example, identifies the innovative aspects of Spaced as a sitcom, but also questions the way such shows, and responses to them, look to distinguish themselves from more popular, 'mass media' sitcoms. Spaced in this sense becomes a symbol for viewers' sense of their own 'cutural capital'. See Brett Mills, The Sitcom (Edinburgh: Edinburgh University Press 2009), pp.132-134.

19. Dan Harries, Film Parody (London: BFI), p.6.

20. Geoff King, Film Comedy (London and New York: Wallflower, 2002), p.107.

21. King, ibid.

22. King, op cit.,p.109.

23. Harries, Film Parody, p.32.

24. James Leggott, Contemporary British Cinema: From Heritage to Horror (London and New York: Wallflower, 2008), p.58.

25. King, op cit., 2002: 123.

26. Wes Gehring, Parody as Film Genre: Never Give a Saga an Even Break (Westport CT: Greenwood Press, 1999), p.7.

27. Simon Pegg, Nerd Do Well (London: Century, 2010), pp.229-230.

28. Harries, Film Parody. p.3.

29. Gehring, op cit.

30. Bordwell, op cit., p.135.

31. See Anon., 'Hot Fuzz', Mirror Online, 16 February 2007, http://www.mirror.co.uk/tv/tv-news/hot-fuzz-452214 ; also Tookey, op cit.

Three: I Kinda Like It Here: *Hot Fuzz* as National Cinema

Throughout this book, I've touched on the question of national identity in *Hot Fuzz*. As we've seen, identifying where *Hot Fuzz* is 'coming from' is not such a simple task: it can't be checked, like some form of cinematic border control, by looking at production sources or noting that the film was partly shot in Somerset. At the same time, identity is central to the way the film is perceived and understood: our conceptions of location and culture, as I've discussed, underpin much of the film's humour. Arguably, a sense of national cultural identity is the concept around which *Hot Fuzz* revolves.

As we saw in the last chapter, though, locating *Hot Fuzz* on any clear side of a notional cinematic divide is not so easy. This is a film largely indebted to the Hollywood action movie, but one that uses this same reference point as a source both of comedy and, in the process, a means of establishing its difference from these same films that influence it. As we saw early on, this is a film that in most respects – location, cast and crew, narrative content – is 'typically English'; but it is also a film partly financed by a Hollywood studio.

This chapter, then, will tease out some of the ideas we've already explored in order to answer the following question: What does it mean to talk about *Hot Fuzz* as an example of 'British national cinema'? To this question, of course, a quick response might be: Does it matter? Surely, some might say, *Hot Fuzz* simply is what it is: trying to work out whether it's 'British' or not hardly makes any difference to the enjoyment of the film. Equally, some might suggest that the question is an unnecessary one, as the film's 'Britishness' speaks for itself. Possibly, if pressed, those saying that the identity of the film is an irrelevance might also be among those for whom this identity is also obvious, and obviously British. This, I suggest, would be to argue backwards, using as a self-evident fact what is, in fact, already in need of proof. In this instance, there seems no question to answer, but only because the answer already *appears* totally natural.

To ask whether *Hot Fuzz* is British is a significant question, if nothing else, for this reason: that our assessments of the things we watch are often unquestioned, made to feel natural and inevitable. It should hopefully be obvious by now that *Hot Fuzz* is not 'naturally' anything; and in fact one of the considerations of this chapter will be what it means to talk about anything being 'natural' at all. As I will discuss, one of the most important aspects of the film is the way it deliberately messes around with conceptions of the 'real' or 'authentic', concepts often held as central to an idea not just of a British cinema, but of 'Britishness' itself.

As I'll consider here, the idea of a national cinema is both explored and ultimately supported by a film like *Hot Fuzz*, even if, or perhaps *because*, it is so complex in its understanding of what this 'national' means. It should also hopefully be clear that this is an important question, especially from a British perspective, concerning as it does how we understand ourselves, and our place in the world, through film. Let me make it clear, though, that what I'm not interested in here is a 'defence' of national cinema. Partly, as I'll argue, this is because I don't know what we would be defending in this instance. But we also need to ask ourselves why we are obliged to defend the idea at all. As we'll see, constructing a defensive idea of national cinema is loaded with problems. This chapter will argue that *Hot Fuzz* manages to avoid these problems; whilst at the same time, paradoxically, pointing to a specific type of British film, in an age when 'national cinema' in its traditional sense has been consigned to the past.

National cinema: 'Buying British'?

What, then, do we need a 'British cinema' for? It's useful to start with the point that, to a large extent, British cinema is not a thing we can actually identify and measure, but a concept, a way of talking about a group of films. Can we really talk about British cinema in the same way we talk about British Gas or the British car industry? Even if we could, what purpose would this actually serve? Actively deciding you want to buy a British car or, let's say for now, British strawberries, is not such a casual act, as it implies either one or both of the following: you like British strawberries more than other strawberries, or/and you wish to support the British growers of these strawberries. In the first instance, Britishness is a kind of character or quality that differentiates one thing from others ('British strawberries are best!'); in the second instance, a specific quality is less important than the idea that something called 'British' or 'Britain' should be maintained – in light, say, of the competition from other 'foreign' growers of strawberries ('Support your British strawberries!').

It's possible that most viewers of *Hot Fuzz*, and maybe you reading this book now, have never given a thought to the health of the British film industry (or strawberry farmers). I'd suspect, however, that in watching this film these same viewers would in some way identify it as British, or at least English. Rightly or wrongly, it's almost impossible not to fall into the tendency to identify a film when we see it, and we often don't need long to locate it in some national terms, whether through dialogue language, the presence of certain actors, or the genre. Whatever the problems involved in reducing a film to one particular place, as if, like a strawberry, it has grown organically out of the soil, locating a film in this way helps to construct ideas of different and distinctive cinemas. And sometimes, our viewing preferences may be shaped by these differences (if, for example, we say we like British films but dislike French ones). Even in these apparently innocent preferences, then, we find ourselves making consumer choices that are in reality part of a process through which one thing is actively valued over another.

All of which points to two apparently straightforward, though in fact very complex questions about British cinema: What exactly is this 'quality' that makes it 'British' and why? And secondly: What is it about this cinema that requires us to value and maintain it, if indeed we need to do this at all?

Problems of definition

One of the challenges confronting many film scholars is to identify a body of films or a tradition representing British national cinema, while at the same time trying to define what this actually *means*. Any number of books recount the condensed history of British cinema in the clear assumption that this is both an identifiable and worthwhile course of study, though many such works inevitably have their own criteria for deciding what this history consists of: be it the economic structures of films produced in Britain; the way in which films 'reflect' society during different periods; or a study based on certain 'auteur' filmmakers, whose main qualification (it seems) is having a British passport. Other approaches have been more probing, especially in the way they consider what it is that motivates both the production and discussion of British cinema, rather than simply take it as a given. But these approaches have also asked important questions about the ways we, as viewers, watch and respond to a range of films, with significant implications for the way we talk about a national cinema.

Andrew Higson has highlighted the way our discussions about national cinema frequently encompass a range of sometimes overlapping but often totally independent aspects. As he puts it, we can discuss 'British cinema' in terms of economics, exhibition and consumption, evaluation or representation. The economic side of things keeps film producers and filmmakers, industry leaders and government representatives busy, focused as it is on the amount of films being made, how and at what cost, and more importantly, what sort of economic returns they are generating: 'From this point of view, the history of a national cinema is the history of a business seeking a secure foothold in the market-place in order to maximise profits, and/or to keep a "national" labour force in full employment.'[32] Looking at things from the perspective of exhibition and consumption is more to do with what audiences are watching, and why, with the further issue of what the British film industry might do to aid its own economic imperatives. As Higson pertinently notes, this discussion has historically focused on the 'assumed effects... of "Americanization"',[33] through the dominance of Hollywood products at cinemas and through other formats. Looking at a national cinema, though, from the perspective of what people are watching (rather than what they 'should' be watching) raises the possibility that 'national cinema' is in fact the most popular one, namely *Hollywood* cinema: a point with significant implications for our discussion of *Hot Fuzz*. The third term, evaluation, is possibly the most problematic, focusing as it does on the idea that a British cinema only really exists as a critically-defined and selected type of film, or the collected work of certain 'approved' filmmakers: 'auteurs'. This approach inevitably has an exclusive or 'high-cultural' emphasis that refuses to consider what many viewers actually prefer to watch. Finally, a representational approach to national cinema focuses on the 'common style... themes, motifs, or preoccupations' shared by a group of films, asking how such films 'project the national character'.[34]

Trying to pin down an idea of any national cinema according to these frameworks carries significant drawbacks. If the support and maintenance of a British film industry, producing profits for British-based businesses and employment for British workers, is a central focus in these discussions, it begs the question where any type of British character or quality comes in. A key debate within the industry in the 1970s and 1980s, during a critical time for British film production, was whether or not British films should effectively emulate Hollywood modes of production in the aim of drawing bigger audiences, both at home and abroad. The question here is to what extent trying to make 'Hollywood' movies 'Made in Britain' renders the British tag an irrelevance, leading us to wonder whether the issue is jobs and profits, and not cinema as an art form at all. For some time, Britain's most significant contribution to international cinema has arguably been as a location for film production and talent pool for film casts and crews. The *Harry Potter* films (2001–2011) are often identified as 'British cinema' for this reason, though they are also major Hollywood studio productions (by, in this case, Warner Bros.), sustained by huge budgets and precisely coordinated global exhibition strategies.

Issues of consumption and evaluation, meanwhile, are connected. Deciding what a national cinema is according to a list of approved films and filmmakers denies the possibility that audiences may identify with 'low-cultural' kinds of filmmaking, but also ignores the fact that for many viewers, their domestic experience of cinema is in fact Hollywood cinema. Considering, finally, national cinema in terms of representation to some extent gets round these problems of judgment; though as Higson observes, such approaches are not without their problems, mainly because they often follow the circular logic I've already identified. As Higson puts it, such approaches 'imply... that cinema simply reflects or expresses a pre-existing national identity, consciousness or culture'.[35] The potential pitfall here is that the 'real' world is constructed in reverse, arguing back from what the films offer us, to the extent that anything can be made to seem a reflection of real national life. Alternately, representations of the nation that do not easily fit within pre-existing ideas of what the nation is or should be like might be disregarded as either fantasy or, indeed, parody. In either case, we need to be aware of the ways films do not necessarily reflect a pre-existing culture – some essential idea of Britain or Britishness – but 'might actively work to produce [new] identities',[36] new ways of seeing the nation.

Parody and identity

If, as I argued in the last chapter, *Hot Fuzz*'s parody does not really have a critical dimension, it begs the question why we need to use the term 'parody' at all. Theorists like Dan Harries, as I have discussed, have drawn attention to the way irony saturates contemporary culture, to the extent that everyone is super-aware of convention, over-familiar with generic motifs, though without that necessarily impacting on our enjoyment of these same conventions or motifs. We are all at once fans, historians and critics of film, who don't need to be told how inherently daft *Lethal Weapon* is, or *Bad Boys II*, because we already worked it out and aren't that bothered. Parody's emergence in recent Hollywood cinema may have helped usher in this era of 'ironic supersaturation', but we are now arguably steeped in it, to the extent that 'straight' films themselves are also at once parodies of their own genres. This is most obvious in the *Scream* films (1996–2011), in essence realistic narratives that nevertheless acknowledge and play around the conventions of the horror genre (and make their parody in a film like *Scary Movie* somewhat redundant).

As we have seen, *Hot Fuzz*'s use of parody plays on an easy familiarity and delight with cinematic and generic conventions, and an enjoyment of their predictability, or indeed silliness. But the other important implication is that 'Hollywood' no longer functions as the 'bad' object of parody – on the other side of which, presumably, we find 'good' British cinema. This doesn't mean we buy into an illusion offered by Hollywood. Like the Wizard of Oz when Toto pulls away the curtain, we've already seen through the smoke and mirrors. 'Hollywood' becomes in this respect a style to play around with, but at the same time it becomes part of our everyday life and perspective. In *Hot Fuzz*, to put it bluntly, it becomes hard to discern the notional boundaries between Sandford and Hollywood. But then, as I'll now argue, the dividing lines between Hollywood and British culture are already drawn in shifting sands.

Where exactly are we?

The scene in which Nick and Danny sit and watch *Point Break* and *Bad Boys II* is in some respects the most believable scene in *Hot Fuzz*. As I said at the start of this book, watching this scene recalled my own varied experiences of growing up (and, I should add, entering middle age) watching movies in similar circumstances. We can most of us identify with this part of the film, especially as for many of us Nick and Danny's vaguely alcoholic slump before the large-screen television might reflect the very same circumstances in which we mostly watch films, including *Hot Fuzz* itself. The use of the television screen (and more recently, the computer screen) as a location around which people gather has of course become a significant feature of television situation comedy, whether this be British shows such as *The Royle Family* (1998–2012) or *The IT Crowd* (2006–2013), or – most obviously – American series like *The Simpsons*. Its similar use in *Hot Fuzz* alludes to some of the more recognisably everyday, intimate practices we ourselves engage in, and this is precisely why so much modern comedy television, which generates humour from the observations of our everyday or familiar routines, should dwell so much on television as a site and object.

Needless to say, shows such as *The Simpsons* have got much comic mileage from turning television into its subject matter. If we spend our lives watching television, *The Simpsons'* logic suggests, our lives become reflections of television itself: this explains why so much of *The Simpsons* works around parodies of the things we see on television, whether these be advertisements, news programming, reality shows, soap operas, television drama, other cartoons, or movies.[37] As Jonathan Gray has noted, the fact that *The Simpsons* is an animation means it automatically, to some degree, parodies what it represents. This is because everything we see in *The Simpsons* that has its anchor in live action is inherently made incongruous, or 'defamiliarised', when rendered in cartoon form. 'Bizarre camera angles; traditional ways of shooting a given scene or genre; devices such as fast editing, panning, close-ups and montage; and even how people move or make facial expressions':[38] all these things that live-action film or television makes seem natural are made to look highly constructed and artificial when shown through the medium of *The Simpsons'* world. *Spaced* is a live-action television series, but what made it seem so novel in the contexts of British sit-coms was that it didn't really *feel* like one. This wasn't so much because the characters talked about *X-Files* or the game *Resident Evil* or *Return of the Jedi* (1983), or even because they watched or played them. Rather, it was because the series was carefully designed to look like them, at least within the remit of a fairly low-budget British television show. *Spaced* was unusual for incorporating within the sit-com format a broad range of televisual, but more prominently cinematic, stylistic techniques: most if not all of the ones Gray identifies in *The Simpsons*. In fact, many of the techniques Wright employs in *Spaced* – crazily titled angles, weird tracking shots, 'crash zooms', quick, unpredictable transitions from one scene to the next – exemplify animation's ability to 'resist notions of the real world',[39] and consequently make *Spaced* as much a cartoon as a traditional 'live-action' show.

Just as *The Simpsons* is (more or less) anchored in a real-world context from which its fantasies and parodies depart, *Spaced* balances its animated flights of fancy within the very mundane contexts of its location. But because point of view and, in turn, our own sense of the show's reality is always blurred and mixed-up, we have no choice but to read the show as representing a world experienced through the consumption and imagination of the films, other TV series and videogames it references. The humour of *Spaced*, and indeed much of the show's warmth, comes from the way its protagonists enact such rich appropriations of their favourite pop-cultural texts in such ordinary surroundings. It is the frequent contrast between 'big' frames of reference (*Star Wars*, *Predator* [1987], *The Matrix* [1999]) and 'little' settings (a flat, paintballing, the local pub) that makes *Spaced* feel so 'local'; even if, paradoxically, this is a result of introducing so many 'global' cultural references into its mix. Significantly, though, none of the references in *Spaced* seem intended for mockery: their use in the show does not signal their failure to mean anything in the 'local' world that is its context; rather, *they change how we understand this 'local' world itself.*

Hot Fuzz is, of course, a film and not a sit-com. But the particular uses of television and parody in both *Hot Fuzz* and *Spaced* suggest different ways of exploring the same thing. In *Spaced*, a television sit-com that is made 'like a film', the site of small-screen everyday life becomes infused with the feel of the 'cinematic': so it is that, at the end of the show's penultimate episode, its two main characters can stand in front of their window in a pose identical to that of Luke and Leia at the end of *The Empire Strikes Back* (1980), while a closing door in the darker foreground replicates the same horizontal wipe that ends that film. The sense of a world lived and seen through cinema permeates *Spaced*, but its characters only occasionally get outside, and – crucially – never go to the cinema, viewing films only ever through the television screen. *Hot Fuzz*, even more than *Spaced*, is about movies, but cinemas are once again conspicuous by their absence. They just don't seem to concern any of the characters here, just as they do not in *Shaun of the Dead* or, later, in *The World's End*, despite the fact that films are a constant source of reference.

This brings us back to Higson's discussion about what we really mean by a 'national cinema'. What *Hot Fuzz* would seem to suggest is that this national cinema – the films we see as people in a particular country – are not obviously 'national' in character, and not even in a cinema. If a popular cinema-going culture in Britain has for a large part revolved around watching Hollywood movies, then the increasing availability of such films on television, and the various media platforms that have followed it, may have only increased this tendency. *Spaced* turns out to have been very aware of the kind of domestic viewer culture it both described and appealed to: one for which blockbuster cinema was part of an everyday domestic familiarity, mixed up with television and videogames, blissfully detached from the economic realities of the 'British film industry', debates about Film Councils and National Lottery funding, or concerns about the virtues of out-of-town multiplexes over local cinemas. Given that the livelihoods of Simon Pegg and Edgar Wright are largely determined by a film industry whose health, for the moment, is still measured principally in terms of box-office receipts, we can assume that the makers of *Hot Fuzz* are not in reality indifferent to these issues. *Hot Fuzz* clearly courted, and attracted, an actual cinema audience that, paradoxically, it does not itself acknowledge; as a Working Title production, meanwhile, it was supported by a company that knew precisely how to make the international business of cinema work for its films. The alchemical formula that made both *Hot Fuzz* and *Shaun of the Dead* so successful, though, was to identify the peculiar make-up of our cinema culture, its mash-up of the mundane and the marvelous.

Perhaps more importantly, *Hot Fuzz* exemplifies a contemporary understanding of film viewing that resists neat categorisations, especially distinctions between 'mass entertainment' and 'art'; between 'popular audiences' and 'experts'. The dominance of Hollywood within a cinematic free market is undoubted, and the sheer weight of distribution and publicity Hollywood can provide inevitably stifles the possibilities of many films to achieve significant levels of exposure. And yet, the often rather elitist attitudes to Hollywood cinema as a form of 'culture industry' selling manufactured fantasy to 'the masses' (whoever they are), or the suggestion that Hollywood represents a kind of 'cultural imperialism' on the part of the United States, underestimates the varied ways many viewers watch and respond to its cinema. The 'saturation' of film culture referred to above, stimulated by the types of multi-platform consumption I've just mentioned, may from one point of view overwhelm us with similar product; but at the same time, it may also have facilitated our development as critical viewers, given the range of comparable material available (including, of course, 'alternative' cinema product which might find their legs beyond cinema releases), and the different ways we are able to watch and even analyse films (the basic ability to be able to rewind or pause a film, for instance, or to upload clips and peruse screen grabs); not to mention the ways that the internet, while giving some people the freedom to air breathtakingly stupid and offensive opinions, has also enabled a kind of democratic discussion forum in which anyone can be a film critic, and not just those authorised by the traditional press.

From 'landscapes' to 'mediascapes'

Media theorist Henry Jenkins first described these practices in 1992, in his analysis of the way fans of television series such as *Star Trek* (1966–9) do not necessarily 'buy into' the obvious (or 'preferred') meaning of the shows, but appropriate them and interpret them in independent ways.[40] Following the philosopher Michel de Certeau, Jenkins described these practices as forms of textual 'poaching': the way in which these viewers take something that does not legally 'belong' to them (not just the characters in a show, but also its ideas, what the show is supposedly 'about'), and make it theirs. Jenkins was writing during a time when most viewers' capacity to make stuff was limited to the production of fan fiction or fanzines, disseminated by post or at conventions, but the arrival both of the internet and cheap means of producing films (digital cameras and editing software like Final Cut Pro) subsequently made the possibilities both much more vast but also more 'professional'.[41] *Hot Fuzz*, like *Spaced* and *Shaun of the Dead*, is not cobbled together from nothing, though much of the ethos comes from a spirit of DIY filmmaking that often parodies or pastiches big-budget productions to frequent comic effect.

When we put these various discussions together, one of the significant conclusions is that the traditional parameters of what makes up a 'national' cinema culture are not so clear-cut. Hollywood might make up the bulk of what film is available on big and small screens, but the ability to 'poach' this cinema and read it to one's own ends undermines its authority to stand for 'Hollywood' as an institution, and its ability to communicate what some suppose to be Hollywood's values or ideologies: rather, it becomes something else to play with, part of the landscape.

But movies, one might say, aren't 'landscapes'. Surely, we might ask, our culture is the places and people that surround us? One simple answer to this is that, well, to an extent cinema *is* our landscape, though maybe 'landscape' is too limiting a word. Let's look carefully again at the setting of *Hot Fuzz*. While the location includes specific sites we can identify geographically and culturally, such as the village square, the church or the model village, some of the most important settings aren't really 'places' in the meaningful sense of the word. In 1995 a French anthropologist called Marc Augé wrote a small but very influential book about what he called 'non-places'.[42] As Augé saw it, modern life, characterised by increasing mobility and the circulation of people and cultural products, meant that the traditional ideas of a 'place', as something inhabited, shared and understood, have changed. Augé's main examples are places like airports or chain hotels, sites that don't have any real sense of identity because they are simply places that lots of people pass through or merely occupy for a short while on their way to somewhere else. But another, and very significant example of this change is the shape and character of English villages and towns. For most of the last century, villages and towns had identifiable centres where people shopped or met. Or people did these things even more locally, on what is now quite quaintly called the 'high street'. Village and town squares or commercial streets still have a distinct look and may be very different from one place to another. Today, though, much of our shopping takes place either in out-of-town retail 'parks' or increasingly not in a physical place at all, but online. Similarly, these commercial centres are also the sites through which we conduct much of our leisure time: eating, bowling (or whatever) and – sometimes – going to the movies. Needless to say, many of these centres, and the cinemas in them, are pretty much the same all over the place: it was outside a cinema like this, in a shopping centre like this, that I saw the poster for *Hot Fuzz*; it was at another almost identical cinema, in another almost identical shopping centre, that I saw *The World's End* was coming soon, just as it would be everywhere else, while waiting to see *Pacific Rim*, which I could have seen either there or in any number of similar places up and down the country that week. Or, like I do much of the time, I could have waited for the film to arrive on DVD, or on Netflix, and watch it from the very un-public space of my living room or office, on a TV, laptop or – more and more, it seems – on my Kindle.

I've already suggested, for this reason, that the scene in Danny's living room is the most believable one in the film, but it's also the defining one in terms of *Hot Fuzz*'s 'world', which is one significantly mediated by other film or television narratives. The other scene that, for me, really makes sense of the film is where Nicholas, driving home to London after his failed attempt to arrest the Sandford conspirators, stops at a motorway service station. Perhaps more than anything else in the UK, the service station (if you're at this moment a confused non-British reader, a service station is where you fill up your car with petrol) epitomises the 'non-place': they all have the same shape, sell the same products, and are all lit in the same harsh fluorescent white light. *Hot Fuzz* captures this marvelously, the sterile illuminated interior of the station matched by the pallid and seemingly life-drained attendant (a nod perhaps to *Shaun of the Dead*'s walking stiffs) asking Angel if there's anything else he can do for him. Angel spies the DVDs for *Point Break* and *Bad Boys II* in a rack, the sign above him reading 'Get Some Action DVDs!' [Figs 21 and 22]. This actually turns out to be the point of narrative transition before the movie's final act, as we see Nicholas literally getting some action, stocking up on sunglasses and spray paint for what turns out to be the climactic showdown back in Sandford.

The first time in the film we actually see a bunch of action DVDs is back in the village supermarket where, later, part of the final confrontation takes place. Angel has just set off in pursuit of the shell-suited shoplifter, when we cut to the more laid-back Danny, reading the blurb on a copy of Jackie Chan's 1992 film *Super Cop* ('Meet the cop... that just can't stop') [Fig 23]. Noticing Angel is running after the thief, Danny throws the DVD down, and a brief shot shows the box landing in a wire bin full of other similar

Fig 21.

Fig 22.

Fig 23.
Hap-
piness...

Fig 24....is
a bin full of
cut-price
DVDs.

products [Fig 24]. Eagle-eyed fans of *Hot Fuzz* also know that if you pause the film at this point, you see at the top of the pile a box for *Shaun of the Dead*, masquerading here as *Zombies Party*.

This may just be one of the many referential 'in-jokes' that pepper both *Hot Fuzz* and *The World's End*, though it strikes me as interesting that Pegg and Wright should associate their first film with such 'bargain bucket' type of cinematic fare. The point is, as the last chapter hopefully made clear, the makers of *Hot Fuzz* take their inspiration from these same films (and rightly so: *Super Cop*, like most of Jackie Chan's Hong Kong films, is great), making their associations with 'cheap' or 'low' cinema irrelevant. When, in the sequence we see from *Bad Boys II*, Martin Lawrence lets Will Smith know that 'the shit just got real', he is stating a narrative fact that blends seamlessly and *Spaced*-like into the world of *Hot Fuzz*. But the use of Lawrence's dialogue is also an acknowledgement of the impact of films like *Bad Boys II* on the 'real' world. Pegg and Wright take the supposed 'shit' of the action genre and make it 'real' in their own way. But they also recognise the strange way that this cinematic shit is in many ways the real of everyday existence. When it comes in the supermarket, itself another 'non-place' of familiar uniformity, like the one in *Hot Fuzz*, this strangeness is even more pronounced. People, as I've discussed elsewhere, like action movies for many reasons, one of which is the intense feeling they provide: an intensity that tends to contrast with the more routine aspects of life as ordinarily lived.[43] More and more, though, these cellophane-wrapped packets of heightened experience – I'm talking about DVDs, not cigarettes, but the comparison is a fair one – find their way into the impulse-buy racks at supermarket cash tills, that most ordinary of ordinary places; the films' promises of sublime thrills pitched besides packets of Tic Tacs and AA batteries. And I'm speaking from experience here: just a few days before writing this present page, anyone spotting me at my local Morrisons would have seen a £5 copy of *The Dark Knight Rises* (2012) in my basket, nestling between the Bran Flakes and my daughter's *Peppa Pig* magazine.

'Another Beautiful Day in God's Country': the aesthetics of heritage

What we used to call 'landscape', then, has been supplemented by other kinds of 'scapes that form the backdrop and foreground to our lives, colouring and shaping our experience in ways that, say, eighteenth-century poets like Wordsworth attributed to mountains or old abbeys.[44] But it's also vital to note that in *Hot Fuzz* the particular uses of the action genre, as we saw above when Angel responds to the call to 'Get Some Action', are marshaled against a very specific type of culture and cinematic/televisual context, one within which a particular conception of 'landscape' plays an important role.

Let's go back to the sequence in the service station. As the scene ends, there is a fade to black/fade up to a new setting. Via a tracking shot from right to left, a country scene comes into view with a sign in the foreground: *Welcome to Sandford: The Community That Cares*. A Land Rover drives down the road, and a soft woodwind melody plays on the soundtrack, in sharp contrast to the more thundering rhythms of the previous scene [Fig 25]. A following shot, moving slowly in the opposite direction, shows the farmer James Reaper looking out in front of two white horses grazing in the field. 'Another beautiful day in God's country,' he says to no one in particular, if only to reassert the feeling such scenes are supposed to inspire in their viewers [Fig 26].

Fig 25.

Fig 26.

Scenes like these are the wholesome country staple of a certain kind of English film and television, and the link made to them in *Hot Fuzz* is an intended one. The unspoilt countryside as a kind of televisual respite within an increasingly urban- or suburbanised society has been a regular feature on UK primetime screens since the 1970s (during which decade colour finally became the norm across all British television channels), starting with series such as *All Creatures Great and Small* (1978–1990), based on the best-selling Yorkshire-set stories by the vet James Herriott. Certainly since the 1990s, the rural drama, often set in the past, has figured as an important part in British TV scheduling, especially for the traditionally popular, family-oriented viewing slot of Sunday evening. The BBC's *Ballykisangel* (1996–2001), shot in Northern Ireland, ITV's *Heartbeat* (1992–), set in 1960s Yorkshire, and more recently on ITV the hugely successful (and exportable) *Downton Abbey* (2010–) have tapped into the fascination with frequently idealised visions of country life; one which is equally catered for by the numerous adaptations of Agatha Christie's Miss Marple stories, about the elderly amateur detective putting scheming killers to rights in apparently dozy English villages.

Heartbeat's premise of a young London policeman relocating to the rural north is clearly part of the inspiration for *Hot Fuzz*'s story, but the spirit of Miss Marple is perhaps more pervasive, as is the very Christie-like *Midsomer Murders* (1997–). The latter is one of the most quietly (and knowingly) deranged shows on primetime television, about a pleasant fictional English shire whose per capita homicide rate is higher than in *The Wire* (2002–8), yet with no noticeable effect on property prices or police presence. The fact that *Hot Fuzz* draws on this same incongruity for its plot, as one person after another is horribly slain by the respectable members of the Neighbourhood Watch Association, indicates the way its parodic reference points cut both ways. In this case, it is the excesses, absurdities and unrealistic nature of *English* television that is here the subject matter of parody.

The instructive lesson of *Hot Fuzz* is that all things are ripe for appropriation, both the 'big' and the 'small', the 'global' and the 'local'. This is because neither of them really exist in any real, material sense: just as the authority of 'Hollywood' is downplayed, so is the idea of a 'real' English place beyond it. But there is, I think, a more serious point to make here, which is that such representations of the English countryside or its pre-urban past arguably *have* been used in such a way as to promote an idea(l) of an 'authentic' English life, one that is in fact far from innocent. Higson has identified what he calls the 'heritage aesthetic' in English cinema (and to an extent television), especially those films associated with the 'Merchant-Ivory' production team[45] in the 1980s and early 1990s – mainly, adaptations of E.M. Forster novels such as *A Room with a View* (1985), *Maurice* (1987) and *Howards End* (1992). These films were made during a period of Conservative Party rule when, as other commentators observed, the idea of a 'national heritage' culture was strongly promoted through an interest in institutions like the National Trust, who own or oversee attractions like aristocratic stately homes that members of the public can visit. For some, this promotion of a national past through relics like these houses, often sold or leased by their impoverished owners, offered an illusion of grandeur and stability in a country that had neither of these qualities, characterised as it was by dwindling international influence, class and racial tensions, large-scale unemployment and urban rioting.[46] For Higson, the 'heritage film' was typified by shots such as the one from *Hot Fuzz* described above: long, lingering shots over landscapes or architecture, allowing the viewer to gaze with contemplative and untroubled pleasure. As Higson puts it, such images 'offer apparently more settled and visually splendid manifestations of an essentially pastoral national identity and authentic culture: "Englishness" as an ancient and natural inheritance, *Great* Britain, The *United* Kingdom'.[47]

Actually, as important a reference point for *Hot Fuzz* as *Bad Boys II*, though a slightly lesser-known one, is *The Wicker Man*, a genuinely unsettling British movie from 1973, set on a small (fictional) Hebridean Island. *Hot Fuzz* owes to this very odd film a significant part of its plot: in *The Wicker Man*, Sergeant Howie, a religiously devout and morally untouchable policeman from the Scottish mainland (played by the fabulously named Edward Woodward, who appears in *Hot Fuzz* as the head of the N.W.A.) goes to the island to investigate the disappearance of a young girl. Once there he finds out that its all-singing and dancing islanders are still calling upon pagan gods to bless their failing crops, though his good detective work doesn't extend to him realising the real reason why he is there: that the missing girl was a ruse to capture him – as required, an authority figure who is also a virgin and a fool – and sacrifice him to the gods in the giant 'wicker man' of the title.

The fact that *The Wicker Man* gives me the creeps owes much to my discomfort in the face of 1970s fashions and folk music, as well as to its grisly plot. Critical opinion is divided as to whether the film is a celebration of more pagan forces over those of law and morality, or whether it's in fact a dark comedy about the lure of those same 'old world' desires (personally, I'm with the guy in the uniform all the way). These debates aside, it seems to me a key part of *Hot Fuzz*'s parodic interweaving of different texts and influences, but most importantly its dialogue with different types of national imagery, that it should re-work the very unfunny story of *The Wicker Man* into its plot: one where a group of figurative 'islanders' – in this instance, what are often called 'Little Englanders' – take equally murderous steps in order to worship to the god of what they call, in a repeated phrase in the film, 'The Greater Good'. In this event, the Greater Good is not the principles of nineteenth-century utilitarian social philosophy, but the preservation of an unchanging little world, free from foreign intervention, where everything is the same and the Village of the Year award remains proudly on display.

Let's go back to the 'heritage' shot described above. Seeing what happens in *Hot Fuzz* once Angel comes into the picture is significant, especially in terms of identifying the relationship the film establishes with this type of worldview. Angel slams his car into the Land Rover before Reaper can make a warning call on his radio. The farmer calls out off screen: 'Mum!' After putting Reaper down with a crisp punch, a gunshot rings out: Angel's head whips round and, in a close-up, we see the aforementioned mother, an elderly lady cocking her shotgun. A burst of kinetic action, Angel running toward her inter-cut with shots of the gun being reloaded, ends with the sergeant leaping up and incapacitating the pensioner with a sprightly flying kick. It should hopefully be obvious to most viewers that kicking old ladies is not a good thing, and if we laugh at this point in the film it is partly because it is so unexpected, but also (I trust) because it is so unreal. But as I've suggested, the point here is that there is no 'real' to take sides on here, just two different kinds of *cinema*. The fantasy of kinetic action cinema is here brought to bear on the different fantasy of heritage, though to say one of them wins out is not really the point. The setting holds the style in check: its element of parody means we can never take its cinematic violence seriously (luckily so).

This balance is important in the film, crucial to its comic touch and lightness, but also its sense of generosity and inclusiveness. Notably, as much as the motifs of British heritage film and television, or rural horror like *The Wicker Man*, are picked at and played with, they – just like the action movies already discussed – form a vital part of *Hot Fuzz*'s atmosphere and narrative form. We might easily forget that much of the plot of *Hot Fuzz* revolves around Angel's efforts to piece together an elaborate crime on the part of Skinner, based around the acquisition of property in the area: a detective story straight out of Christie or *Midsomer Murders*. That he is barking up a completely wrong tree, and that the actual truth is at once more banal and more sinister, owes a lot to the narrative twists of *The Wicker Man*. The film therefore relishes the conventions of these same texts, without taking them too seriously. This is especially important in the context of *The Wicker Man*: the latter becomes another fun film to play with, and just like *Bad Boys II*, it is removed from its possibly more troubling contexts and ideology. Who, after all, *does* take *The Wicker Man* 'seriously'? What would this mean? In *Hot Fuzz*, consistent with its general use of reference and parody, *The Wicker Man* is used for its story and its style, but that is all there is... and perhaps all there should be.

Hot Fuzz's use of both *The Wicker Man* and the traditions of 'heritage' film and television suggest that national cultural identity is a kind of *myth*: in other words, something which exists as somehow true, though in the imagination rather than in 'real life' as such. *The Wicker Man* is an interesting point of reference, in fact, because of its own location within the popular strains of English horror cinema, most commonly associated with the Hammer studios. *Hot Fuzz*, like its predecessor *Shaun of the Dead*, arguably updates (rather than imitates) the type of aesthetic strategies that made the 'Hammer horror' films so successful both at home and abroad. Films such as *The Curse of Frankenstein* (1957) and *Dracula* (1958) were very specific in their intent to highlight the English-ness of their tales, based as they were after all on nineteenth-century English novels.[48] They could only do this, though, by emphasising – or exaggerating – some of the qualities which we might traditionally associate with English-ness: a certain kind of theatrical acting style; a fascination both with the ghostly and with the accoutrements of Victorian science; and especially, a tendency toward lurid and gaudy shapes and textures in the art design, colour cinematography and *mise-en-scène*.

All these qualities we have now come to associate with that largely indefinable, though recognisably 'English' idea of the *gothic*: a mainly literary and artistic tradition with its origins in largely fantastic novels of the late eighteenth century, finding its way into the later works that inspired the Hammer horrors. The gothic is an extremely potent cultural image of a particular idea of English-ness, and an important point of reference for ideas of English cinema: film horror historian David Pirie even goes so as to suggest that the gothic horror film 'remains the only staple cinematic myth which Britain can properly claim its own'.[49] Note again, though, Pirie's use of the word 'myth': the gothic, and films inspired by it, is as much an invention of English writers' imaginations as it is the description of anything that actually exists. However seriously we might take traditions of British gothic horror, and (in Pirie's case) lament its decline, it always represented an attractive *idea* of English-ness. To rethink the argument of one other horror critic, then, 'Gothic excess, self-satire and ironic quotation' may not have been what led to the demise of the Hammer tradition, but the very things that defined them.[50] But as I have suggested in this chapter, and as I'll now conclude, such things do not mitigate against such films' claims as national cinema. In fact, they largely define it as such.

The Holy Grail

Because, as we saw in the last chapter, there is always a critical and reflective quality to parody, nothing is allowed to become too serious. Everything becomes surface and play. In *Hot Fuzz*, as we've seen, this goes both ways. The 'real' world of the English countryside and village is as equally absurd a construction as the tooled-up and frenetic rhythms of the action movie. The concept of 'trans-contextualization' that we considered earlier needs to be rethought slightly in light of this fact. The idea of parody as working through one element (for example, the action genre) being transported into another context (here, English village life) seems clear enough, but it begs the question of how neatly established and distinct these two contexts are in the first place. *Hot Fuzz*'s ultimate point is that neither of these contexts is clearly understandable in any sense of place or identity; rather, they are both mixed up, both as unreal as each other (because neither reflects how anyone actually lives) but at the same time, somehow evoking together the world as we experience it (in terms of the ways we consume cinematic and television texts, and where).

This is a simple and brilliant conception that, executed as well as it is in *Hot Fuzz*, explains much of the film's success both domestically and abroad. What's so smart about the film is that it uses modes of parody in such a way as to enjoy generic pleasures without surrendering to the *implications* of these pleasures (what I have called the 'ideology' of genre). Films such as the Hammer horrors did a similar thing in their deliberately, joyously exaggerated revisitings of English mythology. They, like Pegg and Wright's best work, manage to be identifiably English for the widest possible range of viewers, without being constrained to justify themselves as somehow 'representing the nation'.

This is something of a holy grail for non-Hollywood movies trying to establish a presence on the international stage, though not at the expense of an idea of national identity. A typical bind for contemporary non-Hollywood film-making is to what extent it should 'play the game' when it comes to seeking audiences. Logic would dictate that you make 'big' films to find the biggest number of viewers, but at what cost to an idea of national specificity? It might equally be argued that the pursuit of international audiences is a pointless one: better to keep films, and their budgets, low key, 'domestic' in their focus. But what does this mean in the twenty-first century? And is it strictly true that, by showing an *imaginary* view of modern England, *Hot Fuzz* cannot actually claim to represent its time and place? The point here is that we no longer live in neatly-defined and isolated national contexts that can be easily reduced to clear types of film. There is no necessary remit on what sort of films producers within any one country might wish to make. If within our globalised world there are fewer conditions prescribing what, say, 'English' identity should be, and significantly more factors determining what English identity *could* be, there is essentially no limit on the possibilities of a 'national cinema'.

In any case, as we've seen, *Hot Fuzz* never abandons an idea of its national specificity even in the process of making internationally-exportable cinema. As a parody, we always know where it is coming from, but we need not forego generic pleasures as a by-product. Equally, the film acknowledges many of the contexts of English filmmaking (and television) without ever collapsing, problematically, into an obvious endorsement of some false idea of English place or character. Consistent with parody, as discussed in this book, it holds difference and similarity in balance, acknowledging the continuity of traditions and viewing them, at the same time, with a less serious eye. The result is a film that acknowledges the influence of both Hollywood and the national contexts in a global cinematic age. In the process, *Hot Fuzz* exemplifies a type of commercially viable cinema without compromise, and a type of 'national cinema' that, paradoxically, does not need to assert its nationality.

Footnotes

32. Andrew Higson, *Waving the Flag: Constructing a National Cinema in Britain* (Oxford: Clarendon, 1995), p.4

33. Higson, *op cit.*, p.5.

34. Higson, *ibid.*

35. Higson, *ibid.*

36. Higson, *op cit.*, pp.5-6.

37. See Jonathan Gray, *Watching with The Simpsons* (Abingdon and New York: Routledge, 2006), esp. 43-68.

38. Gray, *op cit.*, p.66.

39. Paul Wells, *Understanding Animation* (Abingdon and New York: Routledge, 1998), p.6 (Quoted in Gray, *ibid.*).

40. Henry Jenkins, *Textual Poachers: Television Fans and Participatory Culture*, updated edition (Abingdon and New York: Routledge, 2013 [originally published 1992]).

41. For more on this see Henry Jenkins, *Convergence Culture: Where Old and New Media Collide* (New York and London: New York University Press, 2006).

42. Marc Augé, *Non-Places: Introduction to an Anthropology of Supermodernity* (London and New York: Verso, 1995).

43. Neil Archer, *Studying The Bourne Ultimatum* (Leighton Buzzard: Auteur, 2012).

44. Arjun Appadurai has come up with the term 'mediascapes' to define this condition. See Arjun Appadurai, *Modernity at Large: Cultural Dimensions of Globalization* (Minneapolis: Minneapolis University Press, 1996), p.33.

45. This has become a recognised shorthand to describe films made collaboratively by producer Ismail Merchant and director James Ivory, though it is often connoted more in terms of a particular style than a body of films.

46. See for example Robert Hewison, *The Heritage Industry: Britain in a Climate of Decline* (London: Methuen, 1987).

47. Andrew Higson, 'The Heritage Film and British Cinema', in Andrew Higson (ed.), *Dissolving Views: Key Writings on British Cinema* (London: Casell, 1996), pp.232-248.

48. Respectively, Mary Shelley's *Frankenstein* (1818), and Bram Stoker's *Dracula* (1897).

49. David Pirie, *A New Heritage of Horror: The English Gothic Cinema* (London and New York: I.B. Tauris, 2008), xv.

50. Steve Chibnall, 'A Heritage of Evil: Pete Walker and the Politics of Gothic Revisionism', in Steve Chibnall and Julian Petley(eds.), *British Horror Cinema* (London and New York: Routledge, 2002), pp. 156-171 (p. 162).

Four: Fanboys in Toyland: *Hot Fuzz* and movie stardom

For good or bad (probably the latter), long after we've stopped talking about *12 Years a Slave*, the excellent film that won the Best Picture Oscar in February 2014, that year's Academy Awards may be mostly remembered as the 'Selfie Ceremony'. I'm referring here of course to the multiply re-tweeted photograph, taken by actor Bradley Cooper, of host (and owner of the phone) Ellen DeGeneres and a bevy of modern Hollywood's great and powerful – Brad Pitt, Kevin Spacey, Jennifer Lawrence, even Meryl Streep – enjoying the moment. Besides the capacity of such images, thanks to Twitter, to become famous not so much overnight as instantaneously, the remarkable thing about this image is the way its immediacy and lack of artifice – the slight fish-eye effect makes Kevin Spacey look distinctly odd – is the source of its appeal. The protocols of Hollywood and its rituals have not traditionally accommodated such behaviour, or more specifically, the public display of this lack of decorum via its own publicity channels. This is because the 'selfie', through the same universal technologies it shares, exposes everyone to the same kind of gaze wherever you are, and is shared in turn by anyone who wants to be a part of it.

I'm not sure if the kind of immediacy and sense of contact engendered by this image, which almost seems to put us on intimate terms with everyone in it – Jen, Brad, Kev, Meryl – is something new in our understanding of stars. It might simply be the latest media variant on our century-old desire to know more about our screen heroes, which began with the first 'fan' magazines, and their photo-spreads of actors at work and play. Thinking about this could provide enough material for several books, and I won't pursue it here. In terms of this present chapter, though, what interests us is the work of actors, and the work of the films in which they appear, in creating and maintaining what we can call star images. Simon Pegg is an interesting example of contemporary stardom because, as I'll explore in this chapter, so much of his appeal comes from the sense that he is 'one of us', and not really 'a star'. As we'll see, though, if Pegg is one of us, how then do we understand what it means to be a 'star' in the twenty-first century?

It is worth pointing out here that no one, I presume, is fooled by the idea that Jennifer Lawrence shares the orbit most of us circle within, her fondness for goofy self-portraits and red-carpet accidents notwithstanding. But the rise of the celebrity selfie, if anything, does provide more obvious evidence of how odd and full of paradoxes the whole business of film stardom is. I will take the approach in this chapter that stars are neither constructed wholly by the various film industries that they represent, nor do they fall to Earth ready-made like some divine celestial body. Stars are in fact produced through a combination of various factors: chance, fashion, the vagaries of film tastes and production, but also – lest we forget – talent and hard work on the part of the individual. At the same time, my approach will also stress how Pegg's stardom owes something to those processes through which film industries *can* shape and determine the star's appeal and marketability. Nor, I will suggest, is a star like Pegg ever free from what I call the ideological implications of the star's cultural existence: the idea that stars must offer a form of reflection and point of identification for the viewer.

This is the paradox of the star: that they must transpose their inherent *extra-ordinariness* into the illusory *ordinariness* of the film's world, so that they may be taken at once for the star *and* the ordinary characters they play.[51] George Clooney, for example, has forged a very successful middle-age career vaguely disguising his Olympic-level, Nespresso-sipping gorgeousness in a variety of 'everyday' roles, with the possible effect that middle-aged also-rans like myself can feel a bit like George Clooney. This is, in fact, nothing new, and is by now such a received idea within film studies it hardly needs to be reasserted. As Richard Maltby has shown, it is a paradox central to the working of mainstream narrative cinema, in its efforts to be at once identifiable to its audiences but also honour its commitment to glamour and entertainment: such cinema, as Maltby eloquently puts it 'has to demonstrate its relevance to the lives of its viewers, to the very lives from which it [thereby] allows them to escape'.[52]

The example of Simon Pegg is an intriguing, if not exceptional one. Pegg emerged in the 2000s as a star of British cinema who subsequently crossed over into Hollywood, without, I think, really compromising this same star persona. Perhaps a good reason for this is that films such as *Shaun of the Dead* and *Hot Fuzz*, as I've argued in this book, are to a large extent already 'Hollywood' movies offset by, or embedded within, British characteristics. When Pegg subsequently appears in more obviously American movies such as *Mission: Impossible III* or the *Star Trek* series he brings with him a strongly developed persona defined through films such as *Hot Fuzz*. Central to this persona is an idea of identification and even proximity, an idea of our closeness to him, which as I've said above are part of many film stars' successful image. But the form this takes in Pegg's work is apparently very different from the construction of 'ordinary extra-ordinariness' so familiar from Hollywood's mainstream production and its stars. Pegg would possibly be the first to admit that he is no Clooney, but nor is he an obvious clown in the tradition of physical comedy performers such as Steve Martin, Jim Carrey or the late Robin Williams. To make the obvious point that Pegg, unlike any of the latter, is English, is still to beg the question whether this makes a difference, and what is it about Pegg's 'English' character that enables him to move so smoothly into Hollywood blockbusters?

Pegg's autobiography *Nerd Do Well* is a useful resource here, working as it does, from the title onward, to create the idea that Pegg is not *really* a movie star at all, or at least one whose success owes significantly to the 'home-grown' values he can and will never let go of (as the inner sleeve of my hardback copy reads, 'NERD DO WELL is the joyous tale of a home-grown superstar and a local boy made good'). The content of the book is similarly split between the desire to ceaselessly reiterate Pegg's fannish sense of amazement and good fortune, especially in terms of all the people he has got to work with, and the consequent reiteration that Pegg is, by virtue of these same factors, a movie star.[53]

Nerd Do Well is at once a modest and honest book, written it seems with a clear awareness that a writer's star stories and location photos are those that sell, but only when they're not obviously self-satisfied about them. Reading more-or-less between the lines of the book's content and structure, that gradually works through his education and growth as a writer and actor, Pegg the biographer intimates what Pegg the screen persona frequently downplays; namely that his success owes very little to luck and, as with most stars, much to ceaseless hard work and ambition. Part of Pegg's skill as a writer and performer is that he makes people *think* he and his characters are one and the same. When I recently taught *Spaced* on an undergraduate course, for instance, it was notable how many students assumed the slacker-ish, sporadically-employed Tim Bisley was a biographical surrogate for his creator, aimlessly pondering life in the years after university and the onset of turning thirty. By all accounts there is *some* truth in this, though as I pointed out to these same undergraduates, no one ever wrote and starred in a Channel 4 sitcom *just* by sitting around smoking 'fatties' and playing *Tomb Raider*. In actual fact Pegg spent the years between graduating from Bristol University and writing/starring in *Spaced* honing his skills and developing his reputation as a comic writer and actor, both on stage and on television (for example, in sketch comedy shows such as *Asylum* [Paramount, 1996] and *Big Train* [BBC, 1998–2002]). If we feel that our relationship to Pegg-as-star is different from most of his Hollywood counterparts, then, this is clearly nothing to do with any absence of professional graft. Nor is it down to any real-world relationship, because the vast majority of people watching his work don't have one. Pegg may not seem like a movie star, but he is a star of movies, frequently very big ones, within which bracket I would even include *Hot Fuzz*. This suggests that whatever relationship we *feel* we have with the star is constructed partly by the particular films in which Pegg appears, but also through a particular construction of protagonist character on Pegg's part.

Understanding both Pegg's work and the cultural 'work' of his star persona, moreover, requires that we are alert to the specific contexts and changing habits of film production and reception. Pegg's persona, especially in *Spaced* and *Shaun of the Dead*, but also in *Hot Fuzz*, fits within a certain type of modern British masculinity on screen, most notably the charming-but-flawed, commitment-phobic male best embodied by Hugh Grant in his various contributions to the Working Title rom-com cycle.[54] As I'll suggest below, I think Pegg's appeal makes as much sense in terms of changing attitudes on the part of audiences towards film and television media, than it does to shifting perspectives on gender. We cannot underestimate, though, the ways in which particular conceptions of gender have contributed to the emergence of actors like Pegg, no longer as comic support, but as leading men.

Man Love

The representation of masculinity constructed through Pegg's early film and television work owes a lot to his creative partnership and off/on-screen relationship with Nick Frost, Pegg's friend since the early 1990s, and alongside Edgar Wright his closest collaborator. The development of this fictional pairing, firstly in *Spaced*, where Frost plays Tim's childhood friend Mike, followed by *Shaun of the Dead*, with Frost as Shaun's slobbish housemate Ed, and then in *Hot Fuzz*, is based around crafted variations on the subject of male friendship. But the depiction of this relationship also indicates an awareness and manipulation of film gender and its use in genre.

The focus on male friendship either as a kind of 'triangulating' effect on a central heterosexual relationship, or as a way of 'disavowing' the gendered implications of male friendship and heterosexual commitment, are common features of genre films – the action movie in particular, or what is often known as the 'buddy' film, of which many action films are also examples – and are key features of the two films specifically quoted in *Hot Fuzz*. *Bad Boys II* represents a familiar strain from action cinema since the late 1980s in its use of the 'mismatched pair': films in which two protagonists are often forced to overcome their differences to work together.[55] As Lisa Purse has pointed out, though, same-race pairings like that of *Bad Boys II*, given the film's predominantly straight male audience, need to deflect or disavow homosexuality (in other words, deny its logical possibility) in a way that the inter-racial pairings of the *Lethal Weapon* or *Rush Hour* (1998–2007) movies – presumably – do not.[56] *Bad Boys II* therefore takes pains to emphasise the heterosexuality of its two main characters (Martin Lawrence's character Marcus is happily married; Mike, played by Will Smith, is secretly dating Marcus' sister). This 'works to mitigate the way in which their bickering often makes them sound like they are "an old married couple"'.[57] But the film is also well aware of the action film's disavowed subtext, as shown by the comic scene in a television store where the pair discuss Marcus's recent accident. In the film's opening sequence, Mike accidentally shot Marcus in the backside, causing some undesired side effects: 'My ass still hurts from what you did to it the other night,' says Marcus in the later scene: 'When you popped me from behind I think you damaged some nerves. Now... I can't even get an erection'. The innuendo is in itself made obvious, but the real comedy of the scene derives from the fact that, unbeknownst to the pair, their conversation is being relayed around the store via a digital camera. As Purse argues, the dialogue between the two men here 'is unusual in its open acknowledgement of the possibility of a lived homosexual domesticity'; but ultimately, the framing of the dialogue shows that this possibility is based on a misunderstanding. The scene therefore 'literalises the buddy movie's homoeroticism while directing us away from it, inviting the audience to focus on the distance between the misinterpretation... and the "guaranteed" reality of Mike and Marcus's oft-reinforced heterosexuality'.[58]

Hot Fuzz, in a similarly 'domestic' and intimate sequence – the aforementioned evening of DVD viewing – also employs innuendo, though here, much more delicately, and with a different kind of framing. In this instance, Nicholas is explaining to Danny that he cannot relax. The dialogue at this point is filmed in a close shot/reverse-shot rhythm, the actors' voices softening as the camera comes slowly closer. Danny gently pokes Nicholas's head, suggesting that he needs to 'turn off that noodle' of his. 'I don't know how,' says Nicholas, pleadingly [Fig 27]. Danny's eye-line drifts momentarily toward Nicholas's mouth: 'I can show you how,' he says [Fig 28].

Fig 27.

Fig 28.

The subsequent shot has Danny get up to reveal, from behind parting screen doors, his vast collection of DVDs. Consistent with the genre, the visual punchline here deflects the 'uncomfortable' connotations of a male-on-male kiss. But the intimacy of the exchange itself is not disavowed: if 'turning off' (and by inference, getting turned on) takes place through watching *Point Break*, this is staged here as the positive *culmination* of the dialogue exchange, rather than an act of negation and denial. In other words, *Hot Fuzz* baulks at giving us an actual homosexual intimacy, a fact which keeps it inevitably within the conventions and gendered frameworks of the Hollywood genre movie. Yet in refusing actual denial, it is arguably more open in acknowledging the homoerotic potential of the genre, both as representation and as a viewing experience. Alluding to the homoerotic possibilities in *Hot Fuzz* without literalising or explaining them actually makes the film quite slippery, refusing (in distinction to *Bad Boys II*) to come clearly down on one side of a homo-/heterosexual dividing line.

This flirting around homosexual pairing, but also (as Pegg has himself suggested) an unembarrassed celebration of 'man love',[59] is a regular feature of the Pegg-Frost partnership. Much of the comedy and narrative in *Spaced* is centred on the relationship of Tim and Mike, the latter eyeing every potential female rival for Tim's affections with near psychotic distrust. Both *Spaced* and *Shaun of the Dead* (which ends with Pegg and the now zombified Frost playing videogames in the garden shed) reaffirm the endurance and comforts of male companionship over – we might argue – the temperamental and often temporary nature of sexual relationships. Notably, though, while it seems that Frost's characters are destined to a life free from romantic entanglements – his characters only have eyes for Pegg's – the heterosexuality of the Pegg persona is constantly acknowledged by his girlfriends; whether these are full-blown romantic interests (Kristen Wiig's Ruth in the later *Paul*, of which more in the next chapter), narrative motivation (Liz, the girl Shaun wants to protect, and win back, in *Shaun of the Dead*), or the middle party (Sophie, the girl who comes between both Tim and Mike *and* Tim and his flatmate Daisy in *Spaced*).

Probably because *Hot Fuzz* is most overtly *about* the homosocial nature of the action genre, it is notably the film where this 'normalising' female figure is absent. A structural gag in the film, perhaps forgotten by its conclusion, is that Nicholas has recently split from his partner, Janine; a consequence it seems of his over-achievement and dedication to police work. In classical narrative terms, this would typically provide a structural motivation for the male protagonist: the successful resolution of the action would be accompanied by the re-achievement of heterosexual union.[60] This is in fact largely what happens in *Shaun of the Dead*, where Shaun's efforts to protect his family and Liz parallel his bid to win back the latter's affection. In *Hot Fuzz*, not only do we never see or hear about Janine again, but we never really 'see' her in the first place: as part of the forensics team in the scene I described previously, she is wearing a chemical suit and breath mask when Nicholas goes to see her, with the ensuing comic results. The real joke here is that Janine is played (uncredited) by the Oscar-winning actor Cate Blanchett, reduced here to a voice and a pair of expressive blue eyes. The film's biggest star, a legitimate Hollywood A-lister, is literally made invisible [Fig 29]; but this is merely the gloss on the bigger and more significant joke that the female is not really 'there' at all in the buddy-action movie.

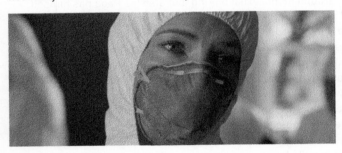

Fig 29. Janine, the visibly invisible love interest

Point Break knows this all along, which is why its gender politics hardly need to be read against the grain. The shared ecstasies of surfing and extreme sports in Kathryn Bigelow's film are exploited here in all their frothy and sweaty appeal, but the narrative makes no effort to deflect its homoerotic charge: the film is about the seduction of one man (Keanu Reeves' FBI agent, Johnny Utah) by another (Patrick Swayze's surfer-bank robber, Bodhi), ending in a foamy fusion of identities on the Australian coast at the film's conclusion, with Utah letting Bodhi catch one final, fatal wave, into which the FBI man also throws his badge. Like in *Hot Fuzz*, the official 'love interest' of the film (Tyler, played by Lori Petty) is little more than a 'token object of exchange' between the two men.[61] *Hot Fuzz* at least makes a pointed joke about the absence of the female character, while *Point Break* simply has Tyler disappear in the last act of the movie, which has its two male leads grapple coitally in free-fall from a plane, one parachute cord between them, Swayze screaming at Reeves to 'Pull it! Pull it!' *Point Break* unashamedly plays out as (in Swayze's own words) 'a love story between two men':[62] *Hot Fuzz*'s appropriation of *Point Break*, while again staying on the 'safe' side of its self-consciously hysterical homoeroticism, indicates its awareness of these themes and tensions in Bigelow's movie.

Whether or not there's a specifically 'national' character to *Hot Fuzz*'s man love is an interesting question, though not one I can really answer here. *Hot Fuzz* is interesting because it is the one work in the Pegg-Frost-Wright *oeuvre* that ultimately makes male friendship entirely self-sufficient. When the great English comedy duo Eric Morecambe and Ernie Wise were on BBC in the 1970s, in a show that revolved around a studio mock-up of their shared flat, one of the masterstrokes of their writer Eddie Braben was to put them in a double bed together, where they would frequently chat before turning in for the night.[63] The charm of this touch was that it contained no sexual innuendo at all, or any kind of sexual content, so it seemed the most natural thing in the world. Braben got the idea from the American comedy films of Laurel and Hardy, though there was often an implication in that duo's work that their relationship was a retreat from hen-pecking wives. In *The Morecambe and Wise Show*, by contrast, women are rarely, if at all, in the picture. It does seem to me of some note that much popular American film and television, when it is not actually exploring a male homosexual relationship, is often hysterical or nervously ironic in its representation of male friendship. *Hot Fuzz* remains unusual in the way it, like Morecambe and Wise, negotiates an alternative path between these two options.

Parody, audiences and stardom

This play on the codes and conventions of the action movie 'bromance', by its own nature, indicates an awareness of these same codes and conventions on the part of *Hot Fuzz*'s creative team. It's tempting to ascribe this to the fact that Pegg studied film theory as part of his drama degree (and devotes chunks of his memoir to reflections both on homoeroticism and ideology in American film and television). But it's more accurate to say that this awareness is structured into the same state of 'ironic supersaturation' giving rise to parody's recent dominance.

As I touched on previously, the older idea that viewers watched Hollywood movies in a state of passive vegetation has by now been systematically countered by various developments in media and film theory. This theory has focused largely on the uses viewers make of film and television texts, indicating their relationship to them is extremely active and critical. As I've argued throughout this book, parody is itself a kind of critical mode of filmmaking, and Pegg's work generally is founded on a highly conscious sense of referential play. As I will discuss, Pegg's star persona is based on a combined, multi-faceted sense of proximity to ourselves as viewers, established through his physicality and performance style, the characters he plays, and the sense of familiarity set up via numerous performances of inter-textuality.

Paul McDonald's work on the Hollywood star system provides points of contact with our discussion of contemporary parody; especially in his suggestion that the new forms of reception, criticism and even creative manipulation of stars and their personae (above all, through the kinds of intervention afforded by the internet), have worked to 'expand the existing discourses of stardom', but also 'decentr[e] the production of star discourses'.[64] What McDonald is essentially saying is that stars and the studios that pay for their services can no longer claim to be totally in control of stars' images. Put simply, we might see this 'decentring' in terms of the way audiences, becoming increasingly aware of how movies work, especially in terms of genre and ideology, are also aware of how much the film star is part of this process, if not the most obvious symbol of it. As an example, think about how much genres such as the action film have traditionally been synonymous with particular (predominantly male, and very 'masculine') actors who supposedly embody the values promoted by the films' narratives.

Once we become aware of what films do, in other words, it is harder to take such star performances seriously. It is not clear whether this, or simply the decline in income for studios, has contributed to the somewhat declining power of the star recently within the Hollywood system. But it is interesting to consider how our more ironic engagement with cinema has contributed to the changing face – and age, and social-demographic reference points – of contemporary Hollywood stardom, and the emergence of stars like Pegg. But it is also important to consider the extent to which these changes, while significant, gloss over the permanence of fairly familiar conceptions of stars and our relationship to them.

Star as Fan, Fan as Star

Most importantly, the appeal of these works, and Pegg's centrality within them, work around the experience of fandom. A lot of Pegg's success, I believe, is rooted in a textual self-definition *as fan*. To a large extent Pegg's 'star-text' – the accumulation of film, television and off-screen performances that make up his star persona – extends to and incorporates works such as *Nerd Do Well*. Photographs and recounted experiences in the book frequently blur the line between Pegg's own experience as fan and his professional work as actor-writer: for example, his interest in comic and sci-fi conventions such as San Diego's Comic-Con, which later interweaves with the filming of *Paul* at the same convention; or his cameo appearance as a zombie in his hero George A. Romero's *Land of the Dead* (2005). But mainly, this idea of star-as-fan is inscribed in the television and film works themselves. In particular, the uses of inter-textuality and parody, as we've seen, frequently draw on viewers' own competence and knowledge as fans of movies, television shows or videogames. What Pegg does so effectively in his first major outing as a lead character, in *Spaced*, is to give these viewers a shared sense of identification through the figure of Tim: an 'everyday' character who shared many of the same reference points and pop-culture-inflected daydreams as, presumably, much of its audience.

As already noted, the paradox of the star is that they have to somehow feel 'close' enough to us through their performances for us to identify with them, but also be attractive and special enough to be differentiated from 'normal' life. The relationship between the fan and the star is traditionally built around this sense of commonality (the star 'speaks to' the fan) combined with exclusivity (the fan can never be like the star, which is why the fan looks up to him or her). Narrative is an important part of this process. In classical terms, a fiction film offers us protagonists and stories that may have the 'impression' of reality that enables us to take the extraordinary (and the highly artificial) for something like ourselves and the world we recognise; while at the same time, the classical fiction film (especially in the high period of Hollywood's 'silver screen', in the

1930s and 1940s) offers us a glimmering world of style and beauty that we can only admire and desire. Because so much of Pegg's television and film work employs modes of parody, though, it seeks to disrupt this institutional relationship between star/text and audience.

Mainstream narrative cinema hides the paradoxes of the star's construction as character. Pegg's work, by contrast, often foregrounds the work of fan consumption consistently, to the point where the 'fan' has displaced the 'star' as the point of identification. Nicholas Angel in *Hot Fuzz*, unlike Tim in *Spaced*, is not a fan: the film actually gets some comic mileage from the idea that he has never seen, or probably even heard of, the films Danny Butterman is so keen to make him watch. But merely *talking* about these films within another feature film calls upon the fan to bring his or her experience to *Hot Fuzz*. It is this move of the fan, from the unspoken figure completing the film experience, to the actual subject of the film itself, that is our interest here. This brings into play the question of what has been called a 'participatory' viewing culture, and one that is an important context for *Hot Fuzz*.

The notion of participatory culture was given prominence in Jenkins' *Textual Poachers*, which as we've seen, was one of the first works to give critical credence to the previously ridiculed world of TV and sci-fi fandom. Jenkins located in fandom modes of resistance to the institutional, hierarchical structures of the entertainment industry. As Jenkins argues:

> From the perspective of dominant taste, fans appear... out of control, undisciplined and independent... Unimpressed by institutional authority and expertise, the fans assert their own right to form interpretations, to offer evaluations, and to construct cultural canons... Fan culture stands as... a refusal of authorial authority and a violation of intellectual property.[65]

Jenkins' case studies in *Textual Poachers* are predominantly examples of the kinds of 'independent' readings to which he alludes here: fan fictions and art works produced mainly outside 'legitimate' production practices, often featuring re-interpretations or imaginative extensions of the subject texts. These texts either exploit inherent ambiguities in their original narratives, or in some instances, stand in open defiance of authorial claims over these stories and their characters. The moment in the second series of *Spaced* when we see Tim, as Luke Skywalker, set fire to his collection of *Star Wars* memorabilia – a direct visual allusion to the end of *Return of the Jedi* – as a protest against the just-previously-released *The Phantom Menace* (1999) is an example of this kind of fan appropriation, here using the iconography of the original *Star Wars* series to actually criticise its first prequel.

It should probably go without saying that the analysis of film stardom from the perspective of Jenkins' *Textual Poachers* is fraught with potential contradiction. This is because the film or television star, more or less by definition, exists on the 'wrong' side of the producer-reader axis that is Jenkins' subject. The star is surely too close to the sources of power to actually assume a parodic relationship to this power. This does not feel like a problem in *Spaced* because Tim's character is so actively constructed as a fan and not a star. But stars, like successful film genres, are always subject to prevailing trends and fashions, and therefore always determined by culture and ideology.[66] While it might *feel* different, the deeper structures that produce and sustain film stardom may be largely unchanged. From this perspective, Pegg's appeal, like that of any star, has very specific historical and cultural characteristics, but it might be rash to suppose that his work and our reception of it radically rethink the production and experience of stars. It does, nevertheless, seem justifiable to suggest it reflects different ways in which audiences relate to film and television texts.

As I've discussed, a central paradox inherent to parody is the way it 'ends up reaffirming' the object of critique through an 'unavoidable acknowledgment of the structure' being critiqued.[67] Parody is always 'double' in the way it reiterates a prior text and indicates quite clearly that it is doing so, and therefore relies heavily on the knowledge and cultural competences of its audiences. But the added quality here relates to the way the parody in *Spaced* or *Hot Fuzz* relies so abundantly on incongruity through relocation. This practice works to situate its protagonists, and consequently its viewers, in a world that is not only very distinct from the worlds of its target texts, but also one that feels much closer to the world of its viewers. Because, then, Pegg and Frost don't look like 'movie stars', and because the setting does not lend itself 'naturally' to an action genre film, we recognise the difference between the context of the film and the traditional contexts and characteristics of the genre. This is of course the same 'gap' between ourselves as viewers and the Hollywood fiction

Fig 30.
Parody
in per-
formance:
so silly it's
almost
believable

film itself that films like *Hot Fuzz* draw attention to. So when Nicholas
and Danny don sunglasses and prepare to hit the pub, the camera arcing
round them [Fig 30], it is hard not to enjoy and indeed identify with the
sense of play-acting fun, especially because the obvious distance between
performance and Hollywood reality seems so far.

A note of caution here, though. As I've suggested, we should be wary of
thinking that a film like *Hot Fuzz* represents something radically new
in terms of the relationship between audiences, stars and their films,
even if it *feels* like it is. The feeling of participation that is an effect of
parody, and an effect of fan knowledge and recognition, does not in itself
undermine the dominant hierarchies separating producer and reader,
filmmakers and viewers: indeed, it is precisely the difficulty of bridging
this gap that underpins Jenkins' focus on 'poaching' as a mode of viewer
activity. As Elana Schefrin has argued in an interesting article on fans
and the *Lord of the Rings* films (2001–2003), it has become increasingly
important within the internet era, where a larger number of fans have
much closer connections than ever before to the producers of films, to
make these fans *believe* in the value and impact of their contributions
and opinions. For Schefrin, though, this 'belief' rarely alters the intrinsic
power structure separating producers from fans,[68] and may in fact be an
important business tool, ensuring fans' support and, in turn, a significant
part of potential audience revenue.[69]

I don't think there's an obvious answer to this problem – if indeed it is
a problem. As I noted earlier, I don't for a second feel that I exist, in the
figurative sense of the term, in the same universe as Simon Pegg, even
if I feel somehow his characterisations, as Tim, Shaun or Nicholas,
make me imagine I know the man, or allow me to see myself through

these characters. This, as I've argued, is an effect of the work's form and narrative, and also owes a great deal to Pegg's skill as a performer. Whatever 'belief' I may have that *Spaced* or *Hot Fuzz* are somehow being created 'by me', in the act of watching them, is again an effect, though one that owes substantially to my own personal experience as a viewer of film and television, and my investment in what Pegg is trying to do through his work. But movies, even if inevitably destined to be entertaining money-making machines for someone or other, are at least significant for the way they represent aspects of our culture, and the way viewers like us play a role in creating this culture. A film like *Hot Fuzz*, along with Pegg's previous and subsequent work in the same vein, if nothing else tells us something about the contemporary status of the film and television fan: especially, the idea that fans 'have moved from the margins to the mainstream', as Jenkins notes in a later revised edition of *Textual Poachers*.[70] Just as importantly, *Hot Fuzz* is typical of a kind of contemporary screen media that is keen to address these same fans: address them in a way that at least allows them to feel like they are contributing to the performance of the finished text. And insofar as an audience is always needed to complete the proper experience of any film – especially *Hot Fuzz*'s form of referential comedy – we could argue that these viewers are, in some senses of the term, contributing for real.

Footnotes

51. See Richard Dyer, *Stars*, revised edition (London: BFI, 1998).

52. Richard Maltby, *Hollywood Cinema* (Malden MA and Oxford: Blackwell, 2003), p.269

53. For example: 'Getting to meet and work with Steven Spielberg was the culmination of many events... and yet, if I could have travelled back in time and told the excitable young boy who had just watched *Raiders of the Lost Ark* that one day in the future the man who created this brilliant piece of cinema would call you on your mobile phone... I can only imagine the sheer joy and excitement that would have consumed me' (Pegg, *op cit.*, pp.12-13).

54. See Andrew Spicer, 'The Reluctance to Commit: Hugh Grant and the New British Romantic Comedy', in Phil Powrie, Bruce Babington and Ann Davies (eds.), *The Trouble with Men: Masculinities in European and Hollywood Cinema* (London: Wallflower, 2004), pp.77-87.

55. Lisa Purse, *Contemporary Action Cinema* (Edinburgh: Edinburgh University Press, 2011), p.134.

56. Purse, *op cit.*, pp.134-135.

57. Purse, *op cit.*, p.135.

58. Purse, *ibid.*

59. Pegg, *op cit.*, pp.146-150.

60. David Bordwell, *Narration in the Fiction Film* (London: Routledge, 1985), pp.157-158.

61. Yvonne Tasker, *Spectacular Bodies: Gender, Genre and the Action Cinema* (London and New York: Routledge, 1993), p.164.

62. In Tasker, *ibid.*

63. See Graham McCann, *Morecambe and Wise* (London: Fourth Estate, 1998), pp. 216-217.

64. Paul McDonald, *The Star System: Hollywood's Production of Popular Identities* (London and New York: Wallflower, 2000), p.114.

65. Jenkins, *Textual Poachers*, p.18.

66. On the relationship between stars, culture and ideology see Dyer, *op cit.*, pp.9-19.

67. Harries, 'Film Parody and the Resuscitation of Genre', p.283.

68. As my colleague Beth Johnson astutely pointed out to me, phenomena like the Oscars selfie appear to collapse the gap between fans and stars, but by becoming global media 'events' reinforce the power of celebrity – and hence the fundamental difference between stars and fans – even more.

69. Elana Shefrin, 'Lord of the Rings, Star Wars, and Participatory Fandom: Mapping New Congruencies between the Internet and Media Entertainment Culture,' *Critical Studies in Mass Communication 21* (2004), pp.261-81.

70. Suzanne Scott and Henry Jenkins, '*Textual Poachers*, Twenty Years Later: A Conversation between Henry Jenkins and Suzanne Scott, in Jenkins, *Textual Poachers*, pp.vii-l.

Five: From Hollywood to the End of the World

This book started life as a short paper I presented, in 2008, at an academic conference on stardom.[71] Much of what I said in that paper has found its way, in some form or other, into the previous chapter. While I was writing that original essay, though, something happened which caused me to rethink what I'd been working on up to that point.

I'm referring to the moment I heard that Pegg had been cast to play Montgomery 'Scottie' Scott in J.J. Abrams' franchise re-boot film, *Star Trek* (2009). I remember reacting to this news with what I can best describe as a kind of vertigo, as the sci-fi fan persona of *Spaced* converged into the very object of his fannish attention. How could 'Tim' be cultishly imitating sci-fi cinema in his own flat one minute, and starring in these same films the next? From one perspective such casting seemed to break the rules, by collapsing the distinction between the mystical place that is Hollywood and the fans that mostly look on from outside. But from another perspective, this was just a hall of mirrors, in which Pegg's persona, and the impression he was 'one of us', made me momentarily forget the actual circumstances of actors' career trajectories (and also the fact that Pegg had already worked with Abrams, on *Mission: Impossible 3*). It's also possible that Abrams, described on the cover of *Empire* magazine in May 2013 as 'the most powerful director in the galaxy', enjoys the irony of casting such an obvious fan: especially one whose *Spaced* alter-ego once said that 'every odd-numbered *Star Trek* movie is shit' (the 2009 film was technically number eleven in the series).

Once we recognise that Pegg's movement towards big movie stardom is a natural one, and that, at the business level of film production, the distance between *Hot Fuzz* and *Star Trek* is not really measured in light years, Pegg's seamless move from film fan to film star should not represent a contradiction. In the case of *Star Trek*, for all its playful reflection on its own status as a reboot, and its gentle acknowledgement of the original series' motifs and structures, the film is too determined by the demands of verisimilitude and dramatic narrative structure to properly accommodate the kind of playfulness we see in films such as *Hot Fuzz*. It remains interesting to me, though, that I could still react with such surprise, and this is surely an indicator of the way *Hot Fuzz* works to brings its audience close, to 'speak to' them in an intimate and familiar way – in a way that *Star Trek*, much as I like it, cannot really do, being simply too big, too far away.

Star Trek is just one aspect of *Hot Fuzz*'s various afterlives, and as suggested above, we can use the former as a way of better understanding the latter. My aim in this final chapter is to look at what happened after *Hot Fuzz*, though I'll do a little more than merely list a set of projects associated with the film's key personnel. Instead, I'd like to consider the ways in which these follow-up films – in this case, *Paul*, *Scott Pilgrim vs. The World*, *The World's End* and, in a slightly different way, *Attack the Block* – all shed comparative light on *Hot Fuzz*, in terms of its particular qualities and the time and place in which it was made. Looking at the first two of these films is also especially interesting because of their more obvious status as 'Hollywood' movies. As the perhaps inevitable destination for Pegg as an actor and Wright as director, it will be useful to analyse the points of similarity and difference between these later films and *Hot Fuzz*.

Paul

Paul [Fig 31] can be seen as a transitional film between Pegg's work with Wright and his new-found prominence within Hollywood. Written by Pegg and his co-star Frost, and directed by the American Greg Mottola (who, amongst other things, directed the hit comedy *Superbad* [2007]), the intermittently deft comedy of *Paul* works around allusions to, and comic inversions of, wider motifs of Hollywood science-fiction film. The Paul of the title is a stranded alien, resident on Earth for half a century. While Paul is the object of fascination and paranoia on the part of the American secret service, he has also secretly been shaping the look and content of American sci-fi television and film since the 1960s. Pegg and Frost here play Graeme and Clive, a budding science fiction artist and writer who run into Paul during their personal sci-fi homage: a road trip of the American west, starting from San Diego Comic-Con, taking in the key landmarks and sights both of America's history of alien conspiracy theory (locations, for example, of alleged alien contact), as well as its sci-fi cinema – films such as *Close Encounters of the Third Kind* (1977), which itself played with narratives and iconography of alien invasion and governmental conspiracies to cover up extra-terrestrial contact.

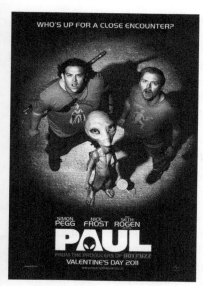

Fig 31. UK poster for Paul

Paul is very much a 'postmodern' science-fiction film, in its recognition that movies are as much about the production and recycling of images as the representation of anything 'real' as such. Hence in *Paul* the alien, with his child's body, huge head and big eyes, resembles the image science-fiction culture has created for it, but then the film undercuts this by mixing his alien-ness with very down-to-earth qualities (Paul is foul-mouthed, laid-back and fond of beer and cigarettes, but also can telepathically transmit knowledge and heal wounds through touch). As a comedy about genre, the film's most obvious predecessor is *Galaxy Quest* (1998), in which the crew of the titular sci-fi television show (very transparently modelled on *Star Trek*) find themselves called upon to fight a very real galactic battle, in a real space ship actually modelled on the television version, for an alien race who have misread transmissions of the show as historical documents. *Paul*, with its dark-suited government agents, also owes a lot to *Men in Black* (1997), especially the way the latter film used science fiction as a way to satirise the inherent weirdness of America itself.

Paul puts fans central to its narrative and, as expected from a Pegg script, offers plenty of inter-textual nods to its audience, with its numerous references to sci-fi iconography. Its effect is very different, though, from Pegg and Wright's collaborations. *Paul* is within the corpus of Pegg's work the most explicitly celebratory of fan culture, largely because it puts Comic-Con into the film itself, with a number of its early scenes shot on location there, and the scenes with Pegg and Frost enjoying San Diego's fan heaven are as much about the spectacular display of the event than any narrative development. As an advert for Comic-Con the film works a treat, but turning the fan event into cinematic spectacle also becomes the film's problem, or at least the thing that makes it very different from Pegg's earlier work. *Spaced*, *Shaun of the Dead* and *Hot Fuzz*, as we've seen, worked by separating their cultural points of reference from their settings. *Paul* is to a large extent about the Hollywood science-fiction film, but it also *is* one, mainly by virtue of its American setting and specific use of geographic icons such as Devil's Tower, the Wyoming landmass that is used so dramatically as the alien landing site in *Close Encounters of the Third Kind*. Interestingly, *Paul* shares the same production details as *Hot Fuzz* (Working Title production, Universal distribution), but its content and tone, and its special effects budget, distinguish it considerably from the earlier film, making it feel much more like a Hollywood movie than *Hot Fuzz* could ever do.

Perhaps more problematically, a show like *Spaced* was endearing for the way the fan in his flat became a type of star. The apparently similar idea in *Paul* here loses some of its effect, as the fan experience of major industry events like Comic-Con becomes itself a kind of Hollywood spectacle, one out of reach to mere mortals. Possibly one of the points of *Paul*, whose road-movie format makes it a kind of documentary of Pegg and Frost's own experience, is that events like Comic-Con are indeed within the grasp of the normal person, albeit at presumably considerable expense. But Comic-Con, frequently used to promote and sell mainstream film and television product, has now become central rather than marginal to the way Hollywood and its subsidiaries in television operate. Bizarrely, then, *Paul* becomes a promotion for the very convention that would be used to promote a film like *Paul*. By celebrating this, *Paul* misses the mischievous sense of distance and imaginative invention that characterised *Spaced* and *Hot Fuzz* and their celebrations of fan activity within very local, domestic confines, far, far away from the power bases of the entertainment industry. What is missing, then, from *Paul* is the playful sense of 'poaching' I discussed in previous chapters, and which are part of the fun in *Spaced*, *Shaun of the Dead* and *Hot Fuzz*.

Scott Pilgrim vs. The World

Scott Pilgrim vs. The World was Edgar Wright's first significant work without Pegg, as well as his first 'proper' Hollywood movie, produced by Universal at a budget of around $60m. The film is based on Brian Lee O'Malley's series of comic books, chronicling the adventures of the eponymous hero in his native Toronto, dealing with the various demands of being a young twenty-something, playing bass guitar in an aspiring rock band and, above all, trying to win the girl of his dreams by taking on her seven 'evil exes' in a number of elaborate face-offs.

Though in some respects a vehicle for Michael Cera, the young Canadian star of films such as *Juno* (2007) and *Superbad*, *Scott Pilgrim vs. The World* is marked by many of the directorial signatures Wright developed in his previous work. The film displays a range of quirky and innovative scene transitions (Wright seems almost allergic to something so simple as a fade in/fade out or an establishing shot), and a now familiar play with on- and off-screen space, cause-effect logic and temporality. Hidden characters suddenly pop up in otherwise 'normal' dialogue scenes, or conventions like split-screen dialogues are re-worked to comic effect. Heads suddenly come into the sides of shots, saying things to characters who instantly find themselves, along with the viewer, in a different scene altogether. At one point, in an unbroken tracking shot, Scott wanders into the bathroom in his house, and comes out into his school corridor. Just as in *Hot Fuzz*, *Scott Pilgrim vs. The World* makes ceaselessly inventive use of the 'language' of filmmaking, creating surprising and arresting movements between shots and sequences, between the time and space of the film's world, without ever surrendering the film's commitment to pace, energy and entertainment.

Wright has said that part of the attraction of *Scott Pilgrim* was that it was a lot like *Spaced*, and this connection is made clear through comparative, and often unpredictable, use of quotation and a playful treatment of screen visuals. Having successfully made out with his literal dream girl Ramona Flowers, Scott walks back through his apartment door to a canned cheer straight out of American situation comedy, and a bass guitar riff like that in the show *Seinfeld*. The fight sequences, meanwhile, are frequently choreographed and visually manipulated to resemble 1990s-style videogames like *Street Fighter* (itself already quoted in an episode of *Spaced*), along with power bars, 'level-ups', running scores and rewards (defeating the various exes, for example causes a shower of digital gold coins to rain down, an increasing amount for each successful victory).

Its most obvious link to *Spaced* though, and also in a way to *Hot Fuzz*, is the way everything in the film is filtered through an inter-textual, pop-cultural imagination that is represented as 'real'. Like the North London flat in *Spaced*, Scott's suburban Toronto home becomes no less real (or no more 'unreal') than his numerous fantastic fights. As in *Spaced*, this is largely because no narrative distinction is made between one nor the other. Scott finds himself in duels-to-the-death with dangerous adversaries because that is simply what happens in Scott's world; and if Ramona has such a group of hostile ex-boyfriends (and one ex-girlfriend) this is simply what comes with the territory. *Scott Pilgrim vs. The World*, as noted above, is based on a comic, and as I discussed earlier, animated forms of storytelling (and the *Scott Pilgrim* books are more figurative and 'cartoony' than more realistic comic art) have a much freer rein to exploit ambiguities between 'real' and 'fantasy' space and time. Given that it was itself an 'animated' live-action show, the choice of *Spaced*'s director for the *Scott Pilgrim vs. The World* film is a natural one; though equally, both *Spaced* and *Scott Pilgrim vs. The World* are related variants on the type of culture-quoting 'geek' culture that has come, if not to dominate our film and television landscape, then at least to have a much more significant presence than it did not so long ago.

Magical Realism

Because both *Spaced* and *Scott Pilgrim vs. The World* make no distinction between 'real' or 'fantasy' worlds, they are examples of what we might call 'magic realism' in film and television. I say this with some hesitation, as the term is more typically used to denote a kind of literary style synonymous with novelists like Salman Rushdie or Gabriel García Márquez, whose narratives frequently blend real and/or realistic places, events and characters with fantastical occurrences in a seamless way. As Maggie Bowers points out, though, some of the literary techniques associated with Nobel-winning novelists like Márquez – talking animals, unexplained transformations, flying carpets – were established features of children's writing long before they became fashionable in the highbrow literary scene.[72] This shared quality, I think, is what makes much of Wright and Pegg's work so refreshing: this sense that apparently incongruous things simply happen, and don't need to be explained away by science or the laws of some alternate universe. It's this that distinguishes their particular fights of fancy from films like the *Lord of the Rings* series, or the *Harry Potter* saga with its (for me, anyway) rather fussy separation between Muggles and Wizards, its strict rules about who can do what and who can't. Such films are about magic, but aren't always as magical as they might appear to be.

If I labour this point it's only to emphasise the type of film I see *Hot Fuzz* to be. As I've suggested here, there is as much if not more 'magic' in *Hot Fuzz* than there is in *Harry Potter* because *Hot Fuzz* is not determined by rules in the same way. Traditionally 'realism' and 'fantasy' are often seen as opposites, when in fact they are closely linked. *Harry Potter* or the *Star Wars* films don't resemble any kind of real life in the sense that I or most people would understand it, but within the terms both series set up for themselves they are perfectly coherent. Harry can't defeat Voldermort just by a whim: he has to spend the best part of eight films growing old and wise enough to do it, and even then he has to spend an age hunting down those pesky horcruxes. *Hot Fuzz*, by contrast, shares with both *Spaced* and *Scott Pilgrim vs. The World* the sense that things in their 'real' world are basically subject to the imagination, to the point where the real world *is* the imagination. We'd be mad to take *Hot Fuzz* to task either for not showing correct levels of police procedure, or for giving us a shootout where no-one gets seriously injured:[73] these things have no place in the film's world and its own physical laws. To a large extent, as I've already implied, they are simply acting out our fantasies of the kinds of film protagonists we might (secretly or openly) want to be, or our own feelings about certain films; only here these fantasies and feelings become the subject of the story itself.

This is also why a film like *Attack the Block*, written and directed by Wright's sometime collaborator Joe Cornish,[74] and on which Wright was executive producer, is actually very far from the spirit of *Hot Fuzz* despite some superficial similarities (including the presence of Frost in a supporting role). Cornish's film, focusing on a group of teenage boys on a South London estate, starts like a piece of 'sinkhole' British realism, as its gang, in a mainly non-violent but no less objectionable way, mug a young woman on her way home from work. A lot of the ensuing narrative focuses on the relationship of the boys, and particularly their leader, Moses, with a local gangster called Hi-Hatz, operating out of a cannabis-growing hothouse in the top floor of the block. The film's focus shifts wildly, though, when it turns out that the area is under threat from some form of violent alien life, and the rest of the film follows their efforts to negotiate both these monsters and the other 'monsters' – crazed criminals, other gangs and, in the end, the police – that they contend with on a day-to-day basis.

Cornish's intent to play out an alien-invasion narrative within the very specific confines of an inner-city estate partly recalls both *Shaun of the Dead* and *Hot Fuzz*, mainly in the sense of mixing genre with location. The film draws on a range of other monster movies, from the first *King Kong* (1933) to the original Japanese *Godzilla* (1953) to the South Korean film *The Host* (2006), all of which use the monster in a largely symbolic way to represent something unspoken in the film: the repressed forces of primitive nature, say, in *King Kong*; the impact of radioactivity in *Godzilla*; the toxicity of American military presence in *The Host*. Location is very specific to all these films, including *Attack the Block*, because the monster – and as I've suggested above, the monster in *Attack the Block* is any number of things – is always linked to its environment. Hence *Attack the Block*'s commitment to a sense of authenticity, through setting and casting, even within the terms of its fantastical premise.

A number of critics noted the ways that *Attack the Block*'s combination of urban realism and collective adventure evoked the spirit of earlier British films such as *Hue and Cry* (1947), where a gang of boys in a still-bombed out East End foil a criminal plot. *Attack the Block* is a significantly darker film, though. No one really gets hurt in *Hue and Cry*, befitting its received status as one of the 'Ealing comedies' made during this period, while *Attack the Block* shows very real effects of violence, including actual death. It's notable that Cornish, who as a white, middle-class boy grew up just outside the type of estate he depicts in the film, went to great lengths to develop the dialogue with his inexperienced cast, all of whom came from the area, and the result is a kind of immediacy in the performances. This, given the various contexts of London urban life in 2011, is possibly what makes *Attack the Block* a significant film of its time.

But its commitment to a type of realism, and its intent to engage on an actual and symbolic level with the social, economic and political realities of the inner cities, make it a very different film from *Hot Fuzz*. Interestingly, *Attack the Block* seems mostly uninterested in the type of reference points so common in Wright and Pegg's work (Michael Brooke, in a very favourable *Sight & Sound* review of *Attack the Block*, criticises Wright and Pegg for 'creating gags around lazy name checks';[75] a reasonable criticism of *Spaced* but overstated with regard to their films). The film's only obvious reference to global popular culture is the moment when one of the gang, bewildered by the evening's turn of events, states his intent to 'go home, lock the door and play FIFA': a line that future generations of film historians may read as a rallying cry for the so-called Generation Xbox. Despite being made by one half (with Adam Buxton) of the *Adam and Joe Show* (Channel 4, 1996–2001), a series celebrated mainly for re-enacting Hollywood films with children's toys, Cornish's film dispenses with the kind of pop-cultural parody that is the DNA of *Hot Fuzz*. This is what gives *Attack the Block* its spiky appeal, though there is a sense for me that the film's realist edge conceals its inherent irony: that it is, in the end, still a genre movie, made very much in the style of one.

Thinking now about *Attack the Block* makes me wonder if I haven't got it all wrong; that my earnest claims for *Hot Fuzz* as somehow representing 'English cinema' in the twenty-first century are off the mark (and if you are an ardent fan of *Attack the Block* and can't quite see the appeal of *Hot Fuzz*, you have my apologies; but then you probably haven't read this far). One of the aims of *Attack the Block* was possibly to offer a vision of its urban setting that to some audiences may itself seem alien, bewildering in its architecture, attitudes and slang – indeed, part of the film's point is that the inner-city young are already regarded by many as monsters.

Needless to say, discussions around the urban inner cities – as a key example, around the time of the widespread rioting that took place in the summer of 2011 – frequently gravitate towards questions of race. *Attack the Block*, with its commitment to a racially diverse cast, becomes a serious sticking point in this present study, because it reminds me what I have so far not mentioned. I have resisted here saying 'never *had to* mention' because this would not quite be true. If we never feel inclined to mention the ethnic composition of either *Hot Fuzz* or *Shaun of the Dead* it is probably because neither film explicitly deals with questions of race, but this is already determined by a cultural viewpoint that still sees whiteness as 'normal' in English cultural life (and by contrast, would see *Attack the Block* as specifically representing ethnic diversity). I don't think this is the place for an extended debate on the issue, and arguably *Hot Fuzz* is to some degree engaged with racial politics. As I argued in chapter three, Sandford's commitment to preserving its Village of the Year status connects it to notions of 'heritage' that are traditionally white and Anglo-Saxon in their connotations. It's also well known that Pegg and Wright have a referential laugh at the expense of the Neighbourhood Watch Association, making their abbreviated name identical to that of the late-80s L.A. rap outfit, otherwise known as Niggaz Wit Attitudes. Nor should it go without mention that Nicholas and Danny find their main source of judicial inspiration in the form of two African-American movie stars.

Equally, though, a certain kind of white, middle-class and masculine worldview runs through both *Shaun of the Dead* and *Hot Fuzz*. From one perspective this is precisely their strength and their point, as it is the weird reality of this worldview that the films explore (and this book has sought to analyse). I'm sure that much of the appeal of *Hot Fuzz* is that it speaks to many of us living in the so-called 'provinces', while also taking a witty and cinematically sophisticated approach to representing it. But it is clearly still a world supported by a fairly privileged and trouble-free existence. So, of course, is the world as depicted by many filmmakers, and like them, Pegg and Wright simply make films about the world they know. In the end we need to admit to these limitations, but also recognise their implications for the way we understand the films.

The World's End

When we come to *The World's End*, the third film in the informal trilogy of films promised, and finally delivered, by Pegg and Wright [Fig 32], these issues come more to the fore. This is because the elements of class, gender and to some extent whiteness are more conspicuous within the

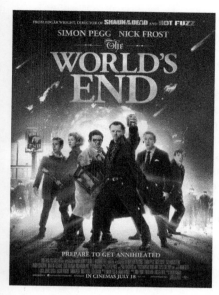

Fig 32. UK poster for The World's End

narrative. Initial trailers for *The World's End* depicted the film as a comic, thrill-a-minute genre mash-up in the vein of its predecessors, with footage of Pegg, Frost and company – Martin Freeman, Paddy Considine and Eddie Marsan joining in the fun – talking about an almighty pub crawl, capering around various boozers, and then battling with freaky humanoid figures. This isn't far off the mark as a plot summary. In the film, Pegg's Gary King, a once-coolest-boy-in-town with his Sisters of Mercy shirt and flowing black trench coat, gathers together his group of school friends in a bid to complete a twelve-pub crawl of Newton Haven nicknamed 'the Golden Mile', the final destination being The World's End. Along the way the group run into old adversaries, old friends and an old flame (played by Rosamund Pike), but also begin to suspect that something is not quite right with the town. Newton Haven has actually become taken over by apparently indestructible alien androids, whose re-attachable limbs bleed inky blue fluid, all of them under the leadership of an unseen presence who describes himself simply as 'The Network'.

As it turns out, *The World's End* is more complex, and not quite as potentially annoying, as its premise suggests. There are probably all sorts of reasons, though none of them obvious, why the film did not perform quite so well as might have been expected, but the simple fact that everyone involved has got that little bit older may have something to do with it.[76] I don't intend this to sound ageist: it isn't (and I'm the same age as Simon Pegg, if that means anything). Age, though, turns out to play a significant part in *The World's End*, in ways that it only implicitly does in, say, *Spaced* or *Shaun of the Dead*, and then only insofar as getting off the sofa and getting a proper job/relationship, and/or saving the world, is a key plot strand. If for the contemporary British middle-class male turning thirty is the point where he decides to grow up a bit, turning forty is often perceived – slightly indulgently – as some kind of personal apocalypse. This might explain the film's curious mix of a drama about men on the official cusp of middle-age, and an end-of-the-world sci-fi action movie; or more particularly, how it blends various crises of ageing masculinity into a narrative of choice, action and redemption in the face of actual global meltdown.

Given that *Hot Fuzz* is in many respects a love letter to the utopian pleasures of no-holds-barred adrenalin rides, and by the same token, to the perpetuation of adolescence into 'adult' life (the obvious recurrent theme throughout Pegg and Wright's collaborations), this makes *The World's End* a more 'grown-up' piece of work. Pegg is actually very convincing as the small-town rebel whose resistance to growing up has left him a deeply annoying but also pitiful figure; while Frost, showing an unfamiliar hardness in his acting range, is particularly good as the former best friend, putting years of irresponsibility and alcohol abuse behind his designer glasses and grown-up professionalism. In fact, *The World's End* is for most of its first half an unnervingly acute drama about male friendship and nostalgia, albeit at some cost to this viewer: I must say my own heart sank when the five ex-friends pile into Gary's car to the sounds of The Soup Dragons' 1990 hit 'I'm Free' – it might be *because* I managed to live through the years of the so-called 'Madchester' scene that any reminder of it has me reaching for the mute button.

Like the other two films in the trilogy, *The World's End* exploits the allegorical potential of its setting and plot. The fictional Newton Haven is an innocuous enough name for a town but is a subtly coded one, at once sounding traditionally 'Old English' but also suggesting 'New Town'. As such, it evokes the types of so-called 'garden cities' or purpose-built towns put up in England between or after the World Wars, often made around a kind of traditional ideal that even Sandford's N.W.A. might find acceptable (though they'd never want to be called a *town*, of course). If anything, though, in *The World's End* this already-nostalgic idea of an English town is positioned accordingly, as it only really exists in the mind of its main protagonist, seen very pointedly in the form of Gary's personal 'home movie' memories (the initial sequence recounting the first attempt to complete the Golden Mile). In some sense the danger posed by such towns, the film suggests, is the unwillingness or inability to leave them, or more specifically the memories of youth, behind. In a perhaps pointed reference to the sort of Friends Reunited and (later) Facebook culture that have helped make nostalgic reunions such a 'normal' part of British experience, the gang meet their various personal Waterloos (unrequited crushes, first sexual conquests, teenage bullies) at a 'School Days' club night. This turns out to be far from the happy and secure 'Haven' it promises to be.

The type of actual New Town most apparently targeted in the film is the conformity and standardisation of English provincial life around safe-but-bland archetypes; the most obvious example here being the sort of pub chains that have tended to replace or absorb the traditional and more independent English public house. Considine's Steven Price comments on this in the film, referring to what he calls the 'Starbucking' of national culture. This seems an odd turnaround from *Hot Fuzz*, which as we've seen appears to celebrate the impact of a more global cultural force on the rigidity of tradition and Little-England mentalities. But this would misread, firstly, the fact that Starbucking is not really the issue in *The World's End*, but rather the dangers of both nostalgia and conformity; and secondly, the point that in *Hot Fuzz*, as I've suggested, forms of 'traditional' English life are not condemned, but integrated into a comic vision of which they are a necessary part. Hollywood and Sandford in the end get along fine, which is why Angel opts in the end to stay, despite the entreaties of his Metropolitan superiors. The ultimate goal for the protagonists of *The World's End* (even Gary, whose desperate effort to complete the Golden Mile appears in aid of psychological 'closure'), is to get out of town for good.

It's significant though that once we discover the secret of Newton Haven, any nuance is overwhelmed by its commitment to a form of sci-fi spectacle, as the androids, brilliant light streaming from mouths and eyes, pursue the humans through the town centre. *Hot Fuzz* obviously takes a similar approach in its final act, but there's a difference here, as *Hot Fuzz*, like *Shaun of the Dead*, integrates its generic spectacle within an incongruous setting to comic effect. Superficially *The World's End* does much of the same, but closer examination suggests otherwise. As we've seen, both *Shaun of the Dead* and *Hot Fuzz* make their generic reference points work coherently within their narratives. Shaun is 'of the dead' before the film even gets going; Nicholas and Danny already inhabit a world where Sunday night television combines weirdly with action-movie mayhem. In contrast, when *The World's End* moves from a middle-aged realist vein to full-blown sci-fi action, the shift feels largely unconvincing, as if tagged on mostly to satisfy the demands and expectations of the trilogy.

The other thing is, we've got very used to this sort of thing in television series like *Doctor Who*. The successful re-boot of the BBC show in 2005 actually kicked off with an episode in which humanoid aliens, the Autons, went on the rampage in a busy shopping centre; indeed, for much of its history, especially in the most recent incarnations of the Doctor, the show has got a lot of mileage out of setting various alien interventions in familiar and often very domestic locations.[77] There's nothing wrong with this, of course, and there's nothing really wrong with its similar use in *The World's End*, only that in the latter it's not that innovative – and indeed, not as wittily explored as it often is in *Doctor Who*.

This is not to say that the themes of conformity, standardisation and nostalgia are not in themselves suitable subjects for science fiction. Beyond *Doctor Who*, there is a sizeable tradition of 'dystopian' science fiction cinema exploiting the cold mathematical horror behind apparently utopian communities. The problem though is that these are not inherently funny: rather, appropriately enough, they are meant to be disturbing. *Shaun of the Dead* and *Hot Fuzz* both work within the terms of their referenced genres *and* as comic films, because both elements are in perfect balance. Even *Paul* is consistent in the way it inverts, in an entirely coherent way, the weird world of alien visitation scenarios. But when *The World's End* tries to make humour out of its generic references, it cannot hold together, because the sci-fi concept is undermined. The ending, for one thing, seems not to take the science fiction element that seriously. Oddly, Gary and his remaining friends defeat The Network by appealing to the same nostalgic teenage ideals that are implicitly critiqued throughout the film (in a truly dystopian moment, Gary actually uses the Soup Dragons' lyrics to combat the alien force). *The World's End*, then, remains a curious and sporadically very interesting film, and a showcase for its creators' range of talents. It's not clear to me, though, that the final result is greater than the sum of its parts. More importantly, looking at Pegg and Wright's work as a whole, their most recent film offers a good example of the dangers in assuming a one-size-fits-all approach to mixing genres.

And now for something completely... similar?

When I started writing this book, it wasn't clear whether there would be any further collaborations between *Hot Fuzz*'s creative team. For good or bad, it now seems that *The World's End* was not quite so prophetic a title, with reports suggesting Wright, Frost and Pegg will come together again soon to work on a new set of films.[78] Perhaps the relatively safe haven and creative consistency of working with Pegg is too big a temptation for Wright after his experiences with Hollywood proper. In 2014 Wright, who had been involved in the project throughout several years of development, was taken off the production of *Ant-Man*; one of the latest films developed by Marvel within their successful superheroes franchise. Possibly the quirky and experimental approach to film storytelling Wright employed on *Scott Pilgrim vs. The World* – an approach which won critical plaudits but did not seem to help the film at the box office – made Wright just too unpredictable a commodity for a Marvel blockbuster.[79]

Whether or not this is true, Wright's travails in Hollywood are a useful indicator of the differences between a big Hollywood production and a more mixed type of production like *Hot Fuzz*; a film which, despite delivering plenty of bang for its relatively small bucks, may have been considered too odd, too risky even, had it been pitched straight to the offices of a major studio. Try to imagine the scene: 'So, it's what? *Point Break* meets... *Midsomer Murders*?'

Footnotes

71. 'Star as Fan, Fan as Star: Simon Pegg and Participatory Culture', unpublished paper given at the conference *New Developments in Stardom*, King's College London, 22 March 2008.

72. Maggie Ann Bowers, *Magic(al) Realism* (London and New York: Routledge, 2004), pp.105-107.

73. Though Chris Tookey's generally hostile *Mail Online* review does exactly this, accusing the film at one point – in an oddly accurate impersonation of Angel at his most pedantic – of not showing an appropriate amount of police procedural work (see http://www.dailymail.co.uk/tvshowbiz/reviews/article-436569/It-aims-It-fires-And-misses.html).

74. Cornish and Wright collaborated on the script for Steven Spielberg's *The Adventures of Tintin* (2011).

75. Michael Brooke, 'Attack the Block', *Sight & Sound* 21.6 (2011), 57-58 (p.57).

76. *The World's End* showed a worldwide box-office gross of $46m on its $28m budget (imdb.com); significantly less than *Hot Fuzz*, which as noted earlier was also a less expensive film to make.

77. See James Chapman, *Inside the TARDIS: The Worlds of Doctor Who* (London and New York: I.B. Tauris, 2013), pp.184-234.

78. See Ben Child, 'Just one more Cornetto trilogy: Simon Pegg and Edgar Wright set for reunion', *theguardian.com*, 20 August 2014 http://www.theguardian.com/film/2014/aug/20/cornetto-trilogy-simon-pegg-edgar-wright-nick-frost [accessed 26 August 2014].

79. Boxofficemojo.com has the worldwide box-office for *Scott Pilgrim vs. The World* at just under $48m, against its $60m budget.

Conclusion: Seriously Good Fun

As I've discussed at points throughout this book, it's the 'straight' approach to the material that makes *Hot Fuzz* tick as a film, as no-one ever comments on how unreal it all is. *The World's End*, by contrast, has its protagonists constantly agog with the far-out weirdness of it all, and oddly – for reasons I addressed in the previous chapter – this means much of the 'magic' dissipates. It's a perennial issue with science fiction cinema, where even the editing between action and the on-looking protagonist – open-mouthed, wide-eyed and incapacitated – is constantly trying to remind us of how amazing it all is (a style perfected by Steven Spielberg in *Close Encounters of the Third Kind*). The one time we see this technique employed in *Hot Fuzz*, revealingly, is when Danny shows Nicholas his DVD collection [Figs 33 and 34]. Excess, typically, is brought back down to earth, though in a way that we can still share and understand as well as laugh at: it is, after all, a *really big* DVD collection.

Fig 33. The 'Spiel-bergian gaze'...

Fig 34. ... and the parodic object of wonder

As I've argued in this book, one of the interesting things about *Hot Fuzz* is that it does not really try too hard to be *about* anything, though ends up revealing a great deal about where it comes from. This is largely because it doesn't feel the need to make any points, nor take itself too seriously. If, as I've suggested, it is in some senses about the peculiarities of English life in the early twenty-first century, it does not need to construct an elaborate cinematic metaphor to do it: one which, like that of *The World's End*, might in any case get lost in the spectacular cross-fire. As a 'British action movie' in the fullest sense of the term, *Hot Fuzz* is already an example of the thing it might otherwise need to describe. Only here, we don't need to have it spelled out for us, or even have to work hard to grasp the concept. It's there for us already, in its playful approach to setting and genre.

Whether or not *Hot Fuzz* is the most interesting film from Wright and Pegg's collaboration, and whether we can call it an *important* British film, is largely a subjective matter. Its unpretentious devotion to giving us a really good time may mean that the film does not figure on too many critics' lists of classic British cinema, or feature prominently in academic books on the same topic, still dominated as many are by the more 'serious' traditions of realism, auteur cinema, or more established national products like the literary adaptation. This is a problem, though. *Hot Fuzz*'s efficiency and ingenuity in bringing together a range of generic inter-texts, and making them work to such thrilling *and* comic effect, makes the film not so much a classic of its kind – what 'kind' would that be, exactly? – but an example of a new kind of smart, film-literate popular cinema.

Shaun of the Dead has deservedly generated a degree of enthusiastic critical response, much of it complimentary of the film's resourceful use of genre and the boost it gave to British cinema at the time. *Shaun of the Dead* is amongst other things a great example of what you can do without huge budgets, and a nifty take on an often over-familiar trope. It also now seems very prescient in anticipating (and indeed encouraging) the more recent emergence of the zombie as a modern cultural icon of sorts. But it also understood what a filmmaker like George A. Romero was doing when he made *Dawn of the Dead*, which was already to use the zombie as an allegorical figure for society in general. The cleverness and quirkiness of *Shaun of the Dead* was to put its protagonists in a pub, while Romero put his band of survivors in a shopping mall, to which his zombies instinctively, habitually returned. The principle in both films, and the significance of the zombie, was the same, only different. This is why

Shaun of the Dead is in many respects a much straighter type of genre film than its reputation might suggest.

There is, though, no obvious precedent for *Hot Fuzz*. Yet such is its ambition, bringing together so many apparently irreconcilable elements, and for it all somehow to *make sense*, it is hard to imagine many films managing to top it. *Hot Fuzz* remains a very unusual and elusive film within the terms of modern popular cinema: a 'formula' movie that is also intricately conceived, crafted and plotted, and therefore difficult to replicate. This accounts for much of its success and reputation. But as I've discussed, it is something more than this. It is an example of what British cinema can do in terms of creating domestically successful and globally exportable cinema without giving up an investment in local specificity, or merely kowtowing to Hollywood's dominant style. And in doing this, it goes some way to identifying where much of its country, and its entertainment culture, found itself sometime around 2007. In my opinion, it does this better than many British films, whether these were seen by more people, were more aesthetically 'challenging', or claimed a more serious realist intent. It's for this reason that we should take *Hot Fuzz* seriously, for all its obvious fun, and recognise its place within recent British cinema history. This book has aimed, and I hope succeeded, to do exactly that.

Bibliography

Bordwell, David, *The Way Hollywood Tells It: Story and Style in Modern Movies*, Berkeley: University of California Press, 2006.

Bradshaw, Peter, 'Hot Fuzz', *Guardian*, 16 February 2007. http://www.theguardian.com/film/2007/feb/16/comedy.actionandadventure [accessed 20 August 2014]

Collis, Clark, 'Brits and Giggles', *Entertainment Weekly*, 18 April 2007. http://www.ew.com/ew/article/0,,20034733,00.html [accessed 20 August 2014]

Dargis, Manohla, 'Banished to the Country, a Too-Good Cop Finds an Action-Movie Parody', *New York Times*, 20 April 2007. http://www.nytimes.com/2007/04/20/movies/20fuzz.html?_r=0 [accessed 20 August 2014]

Fitzgerald, John, *Studying British Cinema: 1999-2009*, Leighton Buzzard: Auteur, 2010.

French, Philip, 'Hot Fuzz', *Observer*, 18 February 2007. http://www.theguardian.com/film/2007/feb/18/comedy.thriller [accessed 20 August 2014]

Harries, Dan, *Film Parody*, London: BFI, 2000.

Harries, Dan, 'Film Parody and the Resuscitation of Genre', in Steve Neale (ed.), *Genre and Contemporary Hollywood*, London: BFI, 2002, 281-293.

Higson, Andrew, *Film England: Culturally English Filmmaking since the 1990s*, London and New York: I.B. Tauris, 2011.

Jenkins, Henry, *Textual Poachers: Television Fans and Participatory Culture*, updated edition, Abingdon and New York: Routledge, 2013.

King, Geoff, *Film Comedy*, London and New York: Wallflower, 2002.

Lane, Anthony, 'Magnum Farce', *New Yorker*, 30 April 2007. http://www.newyorker.com/search?q=anthony+lane+hot+fuzz [accessed 20 August 2014]

Leggott, James, *Contemporary British Cinema: From Heritage to Horror*, London and New York: Wallflower, 2008.

Purse, Lisa, *Contemporary Action Cinema*, Edinburgh: Edinburgh University Press, 2011.

Tookey, Chris, 'It Aims. It Fires. And Yet Somehow It Misses', *Mail Online*, 20 February 2007. http://www.dailymail.co.uk/tvshowbiz/reviews/article-436569/It-aims-It-fires-And-misses.html [accessed 20 August 2014]

Index

Printed and bound by CPI Group (UK) Ltd, Croydon, CR0 4YY

13/04/2025

14656597-0002